...lications for Project Management Leadership

Glen T. Martinez

ABSTRACT

The literature review has proven the percentage of projects that come short of meeting the expectations of stakeholders is significantly high. There is a gap in the literature on attributes that contribute to successful project outcomes, especially in the aerospace and defense industry. This study explores leadership skills in project managers and how the application of leadership skills contributed to successful project outcome. A qualitative multi-case study was conducted to explore leadership skills in project managers within the aerospace and defense industry. A semi-structured interview was conducted to understand the nature of the project that selected candidates participated in and how the usage of leadership skills resulted in successful project outcome.

Table of Contents

LIST OF FIGURES

LIST OF TABLES

Chapter I

INTRODUCTION

Introduction to the Study

The purpose of the study is to explore the leadership skills of project managers and understand how the practice of these leadership skills contribute to successful project outcomes in the aerospace and defense industry. This research study examines the leadership skills of project managers including situational skills, emotional intelligence skills, transformation skills, and relational skills and how they relate to successful project outcomes. Understanding the context and the application of situational, emotional intelligence, transformational, and relational skills could be an essential tool that project leaders use to enhance successful project outcomes (Cerpa &Verna, 2009; Nixon & Harrington, & Parker, 2012;)

This chapter presents an overview of the purpose of the research, a statement of the problem, background of the study, the purpose of the study, the importance of the study, the definition of terms used in the research, and the research questions.

General Statement (Background of Study)

Research shows that projects are failing despite the existence of project management in organizations due to lack of leadership (Hardzic & Durmic, 2015; Spalek 2014). Technology and engineering projects have complexities, unknowns, and uncertainties due to their uniqueness and innovation (Archer & Cameron, 2013; Wilson, 2013; Thermahin, 2013). There are some key leadership skills that are essential in the field of project management to enhance the ability of project managers in achieving successful project outcomes (Nixon et al. 2012; Anca, 2014; Murugesan, 2012).

Situational skills, emotional intelligence skills, transformation skills, and relational skills are known to be an integral set of skills that can equip project managers to successfully manage projects in complex environments (McCleskey, 2014; Pavlou & El Sawy, 2011; Halpin, 2008; Raffo, 2012).

Defining the acceptable measure for project success can be debated and has a long history in the project management field (Gemünden, 2016). Project success could be subjective in some cases based on the expectation of each organization (Rodríguez-Segura & Ortiz-Marcos & Romero & Tafur-Segura, 2016; Muller &Turner, 2010). The fundamental process of assessing project success is by comparing the targeted performance and the actual performance regarding the criteria of schedule, scope, and cost (Gemünden, 2016). Project success is generally defined as the completion of project scope within the constraint of allocated cost, allocated timeframe, and agreed quality. This is used as the operational definition of this study (Rodriguez-Segura et al, 2016; PMBOK, 2013; Blaskovics, 2016).

Project success is typically viewed as successfully completion of the triple restriction called the iron triangle: cost, deadline, and scope. Defining success depends on the type of project, perspective of the stakeholders, and the organization. Project managers are expected to manage projects within the allocated cost, project schedule, and scope defined by the stakeholders (Besteiro & De Souza Pinto & Novaski, 2015). However, project success has extended beyond cost, time, and quality to external factors including future customer demands, stakeholder's expectations, and other qualitative attributes which are also needed for successful project outcome (Rodriguez-Segura et al, 2016). The satisfaction of project stakeholders is typically defined at the beginning of a project, and are in alignment with what the project stakeholders will use to decide if the project is successful (Blaskovics, 2016). In addition to the iron triangle of cost, deadline, and scope, what makes a project successful is the satisfaction of the stakeholders of the project by understanding the strategic objectives of the organization (Rihe, 2007).

Situational leadership skills can be described as the leader's ability to adapt to the follower's behavior based on the specific task and the relationship between the leader and the follower (Hersey & Blanchard, 1969; Hersey & Blanchard, 1979). Situational leadership is beyond task, but well rooted in the ability of a leader to meet a follower's needs and their ability to improve (Hersey & Blanchard, 1969). Situational leadership skills enhance the ability of a manager to work with a variety of employees in the company, which provides the avenue for a manger to evaluate the task and the maturity level of the employee before assigning tasks to achieve the highest possibility of success (Hersey & Blachard, 1979; Luzzi, 2017). The four key approaches that Hersey and Blanchard (1969) described for situational leadership skills are telling/directing, persuading/coaching, participating/supporting, and delegating. Situational leadership skills enhance the ability to diagnose commitment, competency, and performance of others and can be flexible enough to partner with others (Lynch & Lynch & McCormack & McCance, 2011).

Kaminsky (2012) further described situational leadership skills as one of the essential leadership skills that could enhance successful project outcome in project management. The concept of situational leadership is based on the ability of a leader to understand the maturity level of employees and assign projects appropriately (Luzzi, 2017; Lou & Liu, 2014; Cubero, 2007). This leadership skill seeks to reduce emotional conflict, and to improve equal participation through relation orientation (McCleskey, 2014). Situational leadership skills provide depth and flexibility in the organization that is necessary for project managers to adapt to the capacity of employees in the organization (Crosby & Bryson, 2010; Lou and Liu, 2014; Carlos Do Rego Furtado & José Ferreira Silva & Da GraçA CâMara Batista, 2011; Lynch et al, 2011).

The key aspect of situational leadership skills is the maturity level of subordinates and the ability of a leader to adjust to employee's maturity level (Carlos Do Rego Furtado et al., 2011; Cubero, 2007). Adaptability is an integral part of situational leadership, because it explains how a leader can adapt leadership skills based on the current situation (Carlos Do Rego Furtado et al., 2011; Lynch et al, 2011). Versatility in situational leadership skills could be an important skill set that project managers could use to enhance their ability to be successful in managing projects when dealing with multiple personalities within a project (Carlos Do Rego Furtado et al., 2011)

McCleskey (2014) discussed published literature studies that link leadership attributes, including transformational leadership to the effectiveness of a middle manager, CEO success, and military leadership. Transformational leadership can be described as the method to improve and motivate followers through a common integrated goal with a commitment level greater than individual goals (Bryman et al, 2011; McCleskey, 2014; Nixon & Harrington, & Parker, 2012,). Transformational leadership skills have four main attributes: individual consideration, intellectual stimulation, idealize influence, and inspiration motivation. The attributes in transformational leadership are essential for project managers to influence and motivate their team to achieve deliverables and project objectives (McCleskey, 2014).

One of the key essential characteristics of transformational leadership skills is the idealism that a leader can influence followers' behaviors, assumptions, and beliefs, which is highly essential in the field of project management (Moynihan & Pandey & Wright, 2012). Transformational leadership skills enhance the ability of followers to transcend from their self-interest and focus on the best outcome for the organization (McCleskey, 2014). The transformational leadership skill set instills optimism and motivation to encourage team members to achieve a common goal. Idealized influence attributes of transformational leadership skill enable a leader to influence followers through a shared vision (Doody & Doody, 2012).

Emotional Intelligence is an essential skill that project managers must have to be successful. Emotional Intelligence can be described as an interpersonal and intrapersonal skill construct that provides an ability of an individual to control his or her emotions and manage others' emotions (Trejo, 2016; Herniss, 2001; Turner & Lloyd-Walker, 2008). Salovey and Mayer (1989) described emotional intelligence skills as the subset of social intelligence that enhances the ability to monitor other emotions and feelings and one's emotion to guide actions and thought processes. Emotional Intelligence attributes and skills are essential for improving the effectiveness of a project manager and enhancing the success of a project (Trejo, 2016). Day et al. (2008) further contextualized Emotional Intelligence into four attributes, which are: A) the ability to understand emotions, B) the ability to perceive emotions, C) using emotions to facilitate thought, and D) emotional management to enhance personal growth. These attributes are essential for improving the effectiveness of a project manager and enhancing the success of a project.

There are five competencies related to Emotional Intelligence skills: social competencies, empathy, self-regulation, self-motivation, and self-awareness (Turner & Lloyd-Walker, 2008). Turner et al (2008) described the correlation between these EI abilities and successful leadership. Emotional Intelligence skills cannot be overlooked due to the fact that project managers' primarily responsibility is to interact with people and influence them to accomplish project goals. It is implied that people who demonstrate social competencies, empathy, self-regulation, self-motivation, and self-awareness have emotional intelligence skills (Turner & Lloyd-Walker, 2008). The demonstration of EI competencies by project leaders has been linked to job satisfaction, retention, and performance improvement (Turner & Lloyd-Walker, 2008; Herniss 2001). The level of emotional intelligence of project managers is important especially for complex projects due to the constant communication that exists between them and the project team. Emotional intelligence skills would be essential in building trusting relationships between project managers and project teams.

The idea of relational leadership skills and how essential these skills are in the field of project management cannot be ignored. Relational leadership skills can be described as the process of goal achievement and positive change through relationships (Cunliffe & Eriksen,2011; Uhl-Bien, 2006; Raffo, 2012). Project managers have the unique challenge of interfacing with several stakeholders in the organization and influencing each stakeholder to perform activities that will contribute to the success of the program. Leadership can be explained as an influential relationship between a leader and a follower (Silva, 2014; Brown, n.d; Osula & Ng, 2014). Relational leadership skills utilization is driven through effective communication between leaders and followers.

Communication is one of the important leadership skills needed for project managers to be successful due to the level and amount of interaction that they have with multiple stakeholders (Anantatmula, 2010; Anca, 2014). The usage of communication skills could enhance the ability of a leader to articulate the vision of the project and provides the communication channel that followers will use to complete a project assignment (Anantatmula, 2010).

Relational leadership skills are essential for project leaders to develop the influential relationships that will enhance successful project outcome. Raffo (2012) described five attributes that are related to relational leadership skills: being inclusive, purposeful, empowering, process-oriented, and ethical. These five relational leadership skills are essential traits that are important for project managers to successfully lead project teams in accomplishing successful project outcomes.

Practical Problem

The Standish Group (2013) conducted research with findings that show only one-third of projects that were started are successful. The issue of project failure is apparent despite the increase of project management training and skills in the organization. Kaminsky (2012) stated that the failures of some projects are due to the lack of project leadership and not project management. Some project managers lack Emotional Intelligence and situational leadership skills that result in undesired project results, which is often wrongly misinterpreted as a lack of project management or technical skills (Kaminsky, 2012; Cerpa &Verna, 2009; Toader & Adamov & Marin & Moisa, 2010).

Technology corporations tend to focus more on technical competencies rather than leadership skills, which is one of the reasons an estimated one-third of technical projects fail (Standish Group, 2013; Kamsinsky, 2012). Projects fail due to scope increase, being over budget, and deficiency in on-time delivery (Hardzic & Durmic, 2015; Stoshikj et al., 2014; Silvius & Schipper, 2014; Spalek 2014). The necessity of project leadership skills to communicate project vision and manage stakeholder's expectations could prevent project failure due to scope increase and deficiency in on-time delivery (Anca, 2014; DuBois & Koch & Hanlon & Nyatuga & Kerr, 2015).

Statement of the problem

Despite the increase in project management training, research shows about 32% of projects are failing, according to Kaminsky (2012). Projects are failing due to scope increase, being over budget, and lack of on-time delivery to the customer (Hardzic & Durmic, 2015; Stoshikj et al., 2014; Silvius & Schipper, 2014; Spalek 2014). Hardzic & Durmic, (2015) and Anca (2014) further explained that approximately 70 percent of projects fail due to scope increase, being over budget, and lack of leadership skills that could enhance the vision of the project manager to prevent scope increase.

Toader et al. (2010) explained that the percentage of projects that have been cancelled before completion is between 5 to 15% due to lack of consistent progress. Billions of dollars are being wasted every year due to failed projects, especially in software project management development (Toader et al. 2010). The management of an aerospace project is challenging, and there is significant complexity that comes with it. Even though there are guidelines and procedures provided in the design and development of aerospace and defense systems, organizations and corporations still find it challenging to complete projects on-time and within budget. McCleskey (2014) described the relationship between transformational leadership skills as one of the leadership skill sets that could enhance management performance and increase consistent performance. Utilizing appropriate leadership skills could be the key to avoid wasting billions of dollars in the high technology industry (Nixon, Harrington, & Parker, 2012; McCleskey, 2014).

There is an ample amount of pressure that project teams must deal with to complete an aerospace project. This type of pressure tends to cause budget overrun and reduction of quality of the project that is being designed. In most projects, there are multiple reasons why the project fails. Organizations are mainly focusing on improvement of project management skills of project managers without the proactive improvement of their leadership skills (Cerper & Verner, 2009; Toader et al., 2010). It is imperative to understand how successful project managers utilize leadership skills in project management in mitigating the epidemic of project failures in their organizations. This study explores how successful project managers utilize leadership skills during the implementation of their respective successful projects.

Purpose of the Study

The purpose of the study is to explore the leadership skills in project managers and understand how these skills contribute to successful project outcome in the aerospace and defense industry. The ability of a leader to utilize leadership skills in a project is essential to enhancing the success rate of the project (Nixon et al., 2012; Besteiro et al, 2015; Toader, 2010). The responsibility of managing the completion of a project is trusted in the hands of project managers and it is important to ensure that the person in charge of managing the project has leadership skills to successfully lead the project and achieve project objectives (Toader & Brad & Adamov & Moisa, 2010; PMBOK, 2013).

It can be said that one of the main reasons that some projects fail is due to the appointment of personnel who are lacking in appropriate skills to lead the project (Toader et al., 2010).

Project management helps to fulfill desired project outcomes through rigorous management, decision-making, and organizing project activities through planning and controlling (Nixon et al., 2012; Ivory & Alderman, 2005; Anantatmula, 2010; PMBOK, 2013). This is happening while leadership is in the process of guiding project teams to attain project objectives through influential relationships (Nixon et al., 2012; Silva, 2014; Osula & Ng, 2014; Bryman, Collinson, Grint, Jackson, & Uhl-Bien, 2011). Leadership is centered around motivating and guiding people to work together towards a common goal (Anantatmula, 2010). Silva (2004) and Nixon et al. (2012) explained that one of the main characteristics of a leader is to influence followers to achieve a specific goal and vision. This study explores the leadership skills of successful project managers through a qualitative study to understand how they used leadership skills to accomplish successful project outcomes. This research details the specific leadership skills that successful project managers used and how it enhanced the success of their project.

Importance of The Study

This study is essential to understanding the leadership skills of successful project managers in the aerospace and defense industry to improve successful completions of projects due to the complexities that exist in managing a technology project (Maylor & Harvey & & Murray, 2013; Gransberg & Shane & Strong& Del Puerto, 2013; Handzic & Durmic, 2015). There is limited literature available regarding leadership skills in the field of project management in the aerospace and defense industry compared to other industries. How leadership skills contribute to the field of project management is an emerging field of study, but how it relates to successful project outcomes in the aerospace and defense industry has not been fully explored.

One of the requirements of a leader is the ability to influence a group of people to accomplish an intended goal (Silva, 2014; Osula & Ng, 2014). Anca (2014) further defined leadership as a process of goal attainment, which typically exists in a context of a group. Nixon et al. (2012) and Gehring (2007) explained that leadership skills could be taught, which makes the study of leadership important for the field of project management. The literature on the importance of leadership cannot be disputed, which makes it essential in the field of project management (Nixon et al., 2012). Project managers with leadership skills can encourage project teams and stimulate their thinking to solve complex problems (Aga & Noorderhaven & Vallejo, 2016). The leadership style of a project manager is essential not only to complete project responsibilities but also to grow and improve the problem-solving skills of project team members (Nixon et al., 2012; Toader et al., 2010). It is imperative to understand the leadership skills that are needed by project managers for a successful project outcome.

Leadership skills by project managers could enhance the ability to guide project teams in attaining project objectives through influential relationships (Nixon et al., 2012; Silva, 2014; Osula & Ng, 2014; Bryman, Collinson, Grint, Jackson, & Uhl-Bien, 2011). Project leaders with adequate leadership skills could be empowered to be successful in leading and managing complex projects with effective leadership skills (McCleskey, 2014; Trejo, 2016). Understanding the importance of leadership in project management could help the aerospace and defense industry to establish appropriate training that will enable project managers to be successful in leading projects with desired outcomes (Rodriguez-Segura & Ortiz-Marcos & Romero & Tarfur-Segura, 2016; DuBois et al., 2015). Organizations and corporations could accomplish significant improvement in workforce retention, improvement in innovation, and improvement in employee satisfaction due to development of leaders in the organization (Tse & Huang & Lam, 2013).

This study further seeks to understand the leadership skills and traits that selected project managers have used to enhance their abilities to deliver successful project outcomes in the aerospace and defense industry. This study will further highlight the importance of leadership in the field of project management and how project managers can use the associated skills to accomplish successful project outcomes. The research question of exploring leadership skills of successful project managers will contribute to the body of literature and collected knowledge by providing in-depth knowledge on the leadership attributes/skills that contribute to successful project outcomes in the aerospace and defense industry.

Conceptual Framework of Research Study (Nature of the Study)

The framework of this research study was grounded on the exploration of the utilization of leadership skills by project managers and how it affects the outcome of the projects. Successful project outcomes were measured using Muller and Tuner's (2010) project success criteria tool. The leadership skills of participants were examined through interview questions based on the Leadership Development Questionnaire (LDQ) tool as described by Dulewics and Higgs (2005).

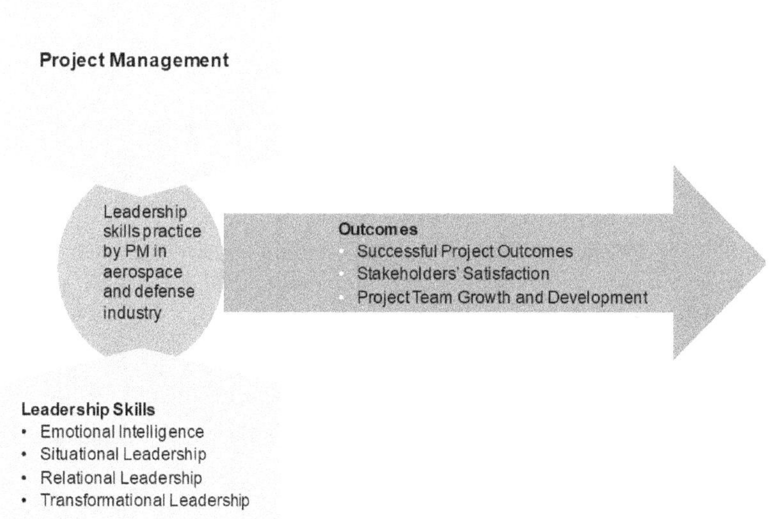

Figure 1 Leadership Skills Framework

Figure 1 describes the conceptual framework of the research subject that shows situational skills, Emotional Intelligence skills, transformation skills, and relational skills as leadership skills needed for project managers to accomplish successful project outcomes. These skills are not only needed for successful project outcomes, but also essential for stakeholders' satisfaction and the growth of project team members.

Nixon et al. (2012) described the importance of emotional intelligence and transformational leadership skills as one of the cornerstones that would improve the success of a project. Situational leadership is essential for project leaders to adapt to the various skill levels that are present in their organization and it provides depth and flexibility in the organization (Cubero, 2007; Luo & Liu, 2014; Carlos Do Rego Furtado et al., 2011; Lynch et al. 2011). This skill is necessary and apparent due to the need to adapt to various people in the organization (Carlos Do Rego Furtado et al., 2011)

Research Question(s)

1. What are the leadership skills, as examined by the Leadership Development Questionnaire (LDQ), in project management that may contribute to successful project outcomes in the aerospace and defense industry?

2. How does the practice of leadership by project managers contribute to successful project outcomes in the aerospace and defense industry?

Overview of Research Design

To fulfill the purpose of this research study, a qualitative multiple case study was used to explore the leadership skills of successful project managers and understand how they contribute to successful project outcomes in the aerospace and defense industry. A qualitative study helps to interpret, analyze, and describe the experience of successful project managers in the aerospace industry (Bazeley, 2013). A multiple case study was used for this research study. A multiple case study has been determined to be the best choice due to the ability that it provides researchers to understand differences between and within cases (Baxter & Jack, 2008). The utilization of a multiple-case study will enhance the ability to analyze differences between multiple cases with the aim of replicating the findings in all the cases (Baxter & Jack, 2008).

The population of research participants was limited to successful project managers in the aerospace and defense industry selected by their employers. There were four project managers selected to participate in the study. These managers reside in Iowa, Illinois, Connecticut, and Oklahoma. The participants met the selection criteria described in Chapter 3 and have a history of managing aerospace and defense projects with successful outcomes in alignment with three triangles and their project stakeholders.

These participants have track records of accomplishing project success and were

confirmed by their leadership. These states were chosen due to the strong presence of

aerospace and defense companies. An in-depth interview was conducted to collect data

on participants' project management experience level, their perception of successful

project outcomes, and to explore their leadership skills.

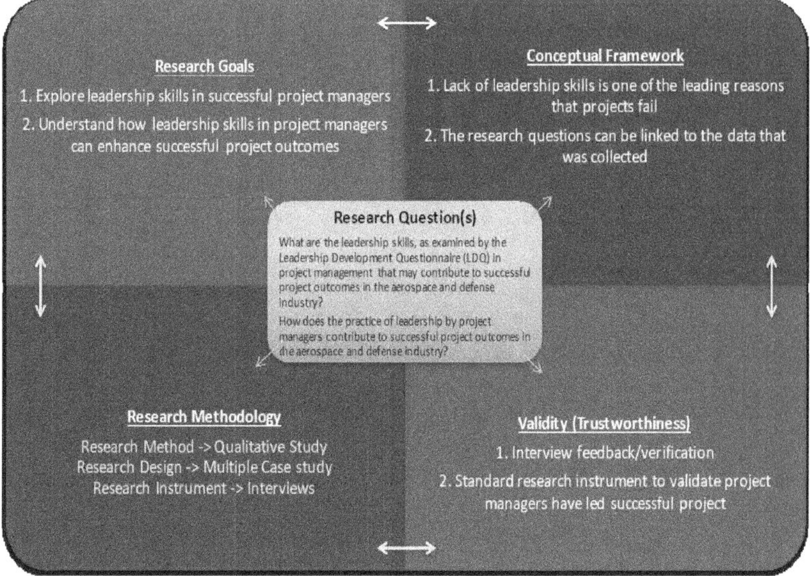

Figure 2-Design Map Overview

Figure 2 describes the overview of the research design for this project, which uses

a qualitative study methodology to explore the importance of leadership skills on

successful project outcomes in the field of project management. The LDQ leadership

instrument was used to explore the research questions in the research design map

overview to investigate leadership skills in successful project managers.

Definition of Terms

Leadership. Leadership can be described as an influential relationship between followers and leaders with the shared purpose of outcome and intended change to achieve a common goal.

Emotional Intelligence. Emotional intelligence is a learned and biological construct that is an essential aspect of interpersonal skills.

Project. A project is a temporary endeavor undertaken to create a unique product, service, or result (Gehring, 2007; PMBOK, 2013; Anca, 2014).

Project Management Office. A project management office (PMO) is an organizational body or entity assigned various responsibilities related to the centralized and coordinated management of those projects under its domain (PMBOK, 2013).

Project Manager. The project manager is the person assigned by the performing organization to achieve the project objectives (DuBois et al., 2015; PMBOK, 2013).

Project Leadership. Project leadership is an ability to get things done well through others.

Transformational Skills. Transformational leadership is to create a significant identification and share a vision with employees beyond rewarding of activity completion.

Relational Skills. Relational leadership can be described as a process that enables leadership in the society to grow through dynamic and theory of relationship to attain positive change.

Situational Skills. Situational leadership skill is the ability of a leader to understand the appropriate response and strategy to employ in a given situation.

Assumptions and Limitations

This research study assumed that four participants included in the research study will answer the interview questions accurately and openly based on their knowledge and experience. The participants of this study were limited to program managers in the aerospace and defense industry, which means that the findings and results are only limited within the context of this specific industry. Lack of adequate technical requirement and planning could contribute to project failure in an organization (Toader et al. 2010; Day et al., 2008). For the purpose of this research study, inadequate technical requirements and poor planning were not considered.

Organization of the Remainder of the Study

Literature reviews have shown the importance of leadership in organizations and the field of project management. Chapter 1 provided the problem statement, background, and the purpose of the research study. The rationale of the study was explained along with the nature of the research that was conducted to explore leadership skills by project managers. In addition to the provision of the nature of research, explanation regarding the research methodology and research participants were provided in this chapter.

Chapter 2 provides information on reviewed literature for the framework of the research. The chapter further elaborates on literature reviews in the area of leadership skills, project management, and successful project outcome.

Chapter II

LITERATURE REVIEW

Introduction

As discussed in Chapter 1, the literature suggests leadership skills are essential for project managers to guide project teams in attaining project objectives (Nixon et al., 2012; Silva, 2014; Osula & Ng, 2014). The purpose of the study is to explore the leadership skills in project managers and understand how the practice of these leadership skills contribute to successful project outcome in the aerospace and defense industry. As mentioned in Chapter 1, literature has described situational skills, emotional intelligence skills, transformation skills, and relational skills as important leadership skills needed for successful project outcomes (Anantatmula, 2010; Anca, 2014; Nizon et al, 2012; Cubero, 2007; Luo & Liu, 2014).

Chapter 2 describes the literature reviews needed to enhance the credibility of the selected research topic. There are articles that discuss the importance of leadership in project management (Hardzic & Durmic, 2015). The literature review in this chapter is mainly based on the research study that was conducted for research topic discussed in Chapter I. This chapter further summarizes the literature behind the research topic and the existing gap in the literature that this research is intending to fill.

Introduction of Topics Covered in Literature Review

The literature review starts with the description of leadership and its importance in the organization. The importance of understanding the conceptual background of leadership is essential for project managers and organization leaders. Knowing what leadership is will help project managers to differentiate between leadership skills and management skills. Adequate leadership skills result in team building and strong connection with followers to achieve a common goal (Ng, 2014; O'Connor & Mortimer, 2013; Silva 2014), which demonstrates an important aspect of said skills. This relationship starts with how individuals in the organization communicate with one another, the trust between individuals, and ethics. Leadership cannot be established without communication, ethics, and trust between leaders and followers. The lack of sufficient definition of leadership skills could cause some misinterpretation regarding the context of these leadership skills and how to efficiently utilize them in the organization.

The next section of the literature review dives into the leadership skills that were explored in this research study. It is essential to understand the current literature reviews that are available for transformational, relational, situational, and emotional intelligence skills. Literature explains the importance of these leadership skills and how they are can be used to influence followers in achieving common goals (Cubero, 2007; Luo & Liu, 2014). The literature explains the importance of these skills and how they can be effective in an organization. The literature also addresses how these leadership skills can enhance the ability of project managers to lead projects to successful outcomes.

Leadership in Context

Leadership can be described as an influential relationship between followers and leaders with the shared purpose of outcome and intended change (Silva, 2014; Brown, n.d; Osula & Ng, 2014). One of the best characteristics of a leader is the ability to influence a group of people to accomplish an intended goal (Silva, 2014; Osula & Ng, 2014). There is a strong connection between how a leader wants to lead and how the followers would like to be led (Bryman et al., 2011; McCleskey, 2014; Osula & Ng,

2014; Bryman et al., 2011). Leadership can also be explained as the ability to influence a group of people to achieve common goals while providing consistent order in an organization (O'Connor & Mortimer, 2013). Silva (2014) defined leadership as the relationship between leaders and followers that is influenced by common outcome or purpose.

There are several definitions of leadership, which can be best interpreted based on the context of an individual or follower and specific interest in the leadership they choose to follow (McCleskey, 2014). It is essential to understand the type of leadership approach that were most effective given organizational and cultural differences that can vary from one group to another (Bryman et al., 2011).

McCleskey (2014) further explained that leadership depends on the interest that followers gravitate towards. Silva (2014) explained that some leaders have no true followers because they were put in a specific position, and followers do not have a choice but to follow them. Leadership relationships should be consensual between leaders and followers. Muna (2011) further explained the core definition of leadership as the ability of a leader to inspire and attract followers. Followers should follow leaders based on positive influence and the vision that is being projected by the leader. Some leaders occupy positions that help to exact some level of influence on follower's due to their authority within the organization. The ability of a leader to positively influence followers is a key aspect of leadership without the use of authority or position (Silva, 2014; O'Connor & Mortimer, 2013).

Some scientists and psychologists have argued that leadership qualities are genetic, which makes it difficult to learn (Silva, 2014). This type of thinking has consistently triggered the discussion as to whether leaders are made or born. Silva (2014) explains a study that used a behavioral genetics approach of identical, fraternal twins that found environmental factors, early opportunities for leadership development, and role models as the reasons behind the variation in leadership and not heredity. McCall (2010) further explained the twin paradigm study that was conducted to understand the impact that genetics has in leadership behavior. The study found that only 30 percent of leadership behavior is hereditary, and 70 percent is attributed to life experience. Leadership can be learned from experience and experience can be transferred or taught through skills development (McCall, 2010). The ability to solve complex problems across a cross-functional organization by government or organization has called for the need for leaders to know a new form of leadership skills (Getha-Taylor & Morse, 2013). Effective leadership skills have become a necessity and not an option, as described by Osula and Ng (2014) due to the flattening of technology and the complexity that surrounds product development.

Leadership practices enhance the ability of an organization to collaborate with an external team and focus on strengths that will complement weaknesses, thereby enhancing the organization's ability to contend efficiently in a competitive environment (Grover & Lynn, 2012). Ansell and Gash (2012) further explained the important role of leadership in creating and realizing opportunities that will add value to stakeholders. Leaders are typically called upon to play a pivotal role in ensuring that the need of the people involved in system or function is met. Silva (2014) and McCall (2010) explained that leadership attributes can be treated as a set of skills that can be learned and fully developed like any other skill set.

Leadership Skills

Emotional Intelligence Skill

Emotional intelligence is an essential aspect of successful project management. Emotional intelligence is a learned and biological construct that is an essential aspect of interpersonal skills (Trejo, 2016; Herniss, 2001; Salovey & Mayer, 1989; Turner & Lloyd-Walker, 2008). It is imperative for a project manager to not only manage his/her own emotions, but to manage others' emotions as well. Trejo (2016) described emotional intelligence as the ability of a person to control his or her emotions and accurately interpret emotions of other people. The conceptual rationale behind emotional intelligence is to gain a social construct on the implication of one's own emotions and the feelings of others (Trejo, 2016). Mastering the skills of emotional intelligence will facilitate the ability of a leader to be pragmatic about the leadership strategy, based on the reaction of the follower. Project managers work with individuals with different backgrounds in a cross-functional organization. The ability of an individual to know personal emotional states will increase a leader's self-awareness (Day et al., 2008). Self-awareness will help leaders to understand self-worth, which will improve self-efficacy in the process of project leadership.

A project manager should have the ability to create a conducive, emotional environment that maintains the morale of his/her followers and facilitates innovation to solve complex problems. One important aspect of being a project manager is the ability to cope with different situations, while being charismatic in the process. Turner and Lloyd-Walker (2008) explained the correlation between leaders who can regulate their emotions with the ability to manage the moods of their followers. Trejo (2016) described people with high emotional intelligence as having the ability to exhibit a positive emotional outlook to reduce the amount of negativity in the organization.

When a project manager creates a positive environment in the organization, it facilitates the relationship between team members, improves personal growth, and increases self-acceptance in the organization (Turner & Lloyd-Walker, 2008; Trejo, 2016). There have been several studies that have described emotional intelligence abilities as a good indicator of the level of performance of employees in an organization (Trejo, 2016). Therefore, the ability of a project manager to understand his or her own emotions and control the emotions of the employees is essential for the success of projects in the organization (Turner & Lloyd-Walker, 2008; Trejo, 2016;). It can be said that a project manager could potentially enhance his or her leadership abilities by understanding his or her emotional intelligence competency level

Trejo (2016) explained a research study that was conducted with 88 people working on a technical project. The purpose of this study was to explore the relationship between emotional intelligence and project outcome. The results of the research support the hypothesis of a significant positive relationship between high emotional intelligence and positive project outcomes (Trejo, 2016). It can be said that organizations are highly recommended to integrate the development program of emotional intelligence as a skill set for managers and project managers.

The importance of emotional intelligence in organizational effectiveness is essential due to the impact that managers have in the emotional state of employees. Herniss (2001) explained the correlation between emotional intelligence skills in managers and employee retention. The path to organizational effectiveness is related to managing self-emotions and the emotions of other employees. Emotional intelligence is centered around the relationship, and the implementation of these skills could affect the quality of a relationship (Herniss, 2001). The relationship between a project manager and employees is essential due to the impact it has on employee retention in the organization.

Project managers' emotional intelligence is critical when managing project activities due to the level of influence it has on project team members. The complexity of a specific project could create a tense emotional state for team members, which would require a project manager to demonstrate emotional intelligence that would motivate team members and encourage them to work together. Emotional intelligence is essential in building a relationship between project managers and employees (Herniss, 2001). The relationship between project managers and employees is related to the development of talents within a project team and how they contribute to the team. Individual emotional intelligence by project managers is important to propel the emotional intelligence of a project team. Group-level emotional intelligence fosters creativity, commitment, and cooperation that could enhance organizational effectiveness (Herniss, 2001).

There is a high probability of conflict in a complex project. Handling conflict is an important skill that project managers must have, according to Archer and Cameron (2013). Due to the likelihood of difference in objective during collaboration and project execution, there is a possibility of conflict with people who are involved in the project. Conflict is one of the attributes that can undermine the successful outcome of a project and having the ability to effectively mediate conflicted situations is an important skill that project managers should possess (Ansell & Gash, 2012; Miller & Balaputia & Sesay, 2015).

Situational Leadership Skill

Situational leadership skill means the ability of a leader to understand the appropriate response and strategy to employ in any given situation (Lynch et al., 2011; McCleskey, 2014). Situational leadership encourages a leader to see each task or situation differently and modify his or her leadership strategy based on a given task or situation. One important aspect of situational leadership, as described by McCleskey (2014), is the ability to correlate the leadership style to the maturity level of the followers. Possessing situational leadership skill is essential in the field of project management due to the cross-functional interaction that project managers must exercise on a daily basis.

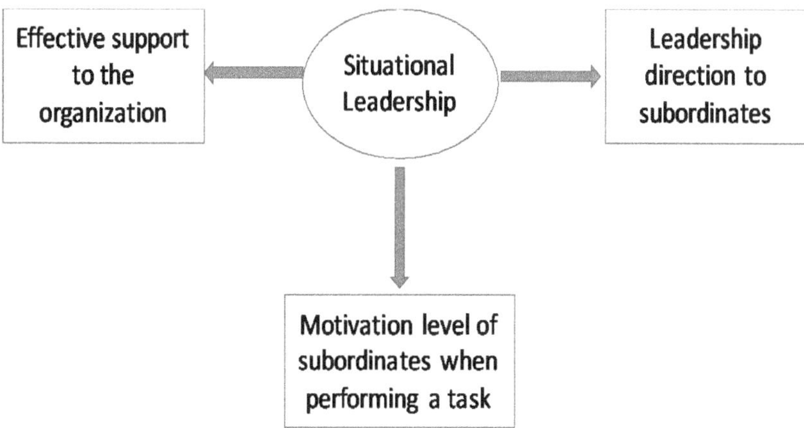

Figure 3 Situational Leadership and Subordinate Support

It is important for a project manager to be pragmatic with his or her leadership style and adjust it on an individual or situational basis to get the best possible outcome. Project managers interact with personnel who have diverse backgrounds and different levels of understanding. Clarke (2012) explained that all projects are not the same and have different areas of dimension. The differences in projects confirm the need for flexibility in the field of project management. It is important to understand how to effectively relate to individuals in the organization.

McCleskey (2014) explained the situational leadership approach is needed to correlate leader ability to the maturity of the follower. Project managers have the opportunity to interact with all levels of the organization, from the executive level to the junior level. The degree of maturity and experience of people in these levels is different, and it will take situational leadership skills to understand the appropriate type of leadership that will work with each member of the project team (Lou & Liu, 2014; Lynch et al., 2011). Situational leadership strategy is different from other leadership theory because it is behavioral and heavily focuses on how to adapt to the situation with the follower. One of the goals of situational leadership is to assist managers to efficiently communicate with their employees and to help with their commitment and competence while acknowledging their differences (Farmer, 2005).

Situational Leadership Skills and Dynamic Capabilities

Situational leadership skill provides the avenue for project managers to have dynamic capabilities while managing a complex project. Helfat and Peteraf (2009) explained one of the concepts and abilities of dynamic capabilities is to maintain an organization's competitive advantage by quickly responding to change and augmenting its strategy to accommodate the change. Project managers need dynamic capability skill due to unexpected changes that happen through the course of the project. Dynamic capabilities explore the functional competence, resources, and organizational skills for alteration of strategic change to create a new capability of operation for quick decision making (Helfat & Peteraf, 2009; Pavlou & El Sawy, 2011).

Dynamic capabilities align and modify resources for exploitation to facilitate learning and collaboration, which will result in the exploration that will sustain the organization in the future (Nooteboom 2010). This learning is what will give birth to opportunities that can be externally explored and enhance successful completion of a given project. Project leaders in organizations have difficulties in making a good decision in a tough management environment due to complexity. Helfat and Peteraf (2009) explained that there has to be a desire or purpose for the leaders in the organization to change or exploit assets in an organization. This form of resource exploitation cannot be attributed to luck or coincidence, but must be a deliberate or purposeful act that will show intention. Pavlou and El Sawy (2011) described the purpose of dynamic capabilities as a process that will help organizations to modify, extend, and manage assets for appropriate reaction to turbulence with the use of existing capabilities. The ability to improve and further the knowledge of how leadership skills contribute to successful project outcome is engraved in understanding the type of leadership traits that fit a given team or work best for a specific project (Clarke 2012).

The ability to change and respond to change is one of the most important attributes of dynamic capabilities, which results in a competitive advantage for an organization (Helfat & Peteraf, 2009; Nooteboom 2010). Helfat and Peteraf (2009) described dynamic capabilities as the process of purposefully modifying, creating, and extending available resources in the organization. Self-awareness is needed by the leadership of the organization to purposefully create, change, or modify the resources that are available in the organization. The modification of this type of resource is needed to respond to an external or internal change for competitive advantage or to prevent an external threat to the organization. The altering and modification of internal resources

cannot be accomplished without a deep knowledge of the culture and talent that resides in

the organization. It is essential to differentiate between the competitive advantage that

dynamic capabilities bring to the organization and how an organization can leverage the

advantages. The concept of dynamic is engraved in having resources aligned and ready

for an environment change and use the change for a competitive advantage.

What brings the competitive advantage through the implementation of dynamic

capabilities is the readiness of assets allocation that exist compared to other organizations

that do not have these asset allocations. Pavlou and El Sawy (2011) explained four

attributes of dynamic capabilities, which are sensing capability, learning capability,

integrating capability, and coordinating capability. Sensing capability can be described

as the process of scanning and realizing opportunities in the environment to attain

sustainability (Pavlou & El Sawy, 2011). This aspect of dynamic capability can be

associated with and related to strategic exploration, as described by Nooteboom (2010)

when discussing how an organization can achieve long-term sustainability during

scanning for external opportunities.   Learning capability is the process of using existing

knowledge to generate new capabilities (Pavlou & El Sawy, 2011). The ability to learn

and then having flexibility to generate the learning into a new capability is an integral

aspect of dynamic capabilities.

Pavlou and El Sawy (2011) described dynamic capability as the process of

integrating new capabilities into an existing knowledge. The integration of these

capabilities is essential to manage the environmental change that will give an

organization a competitive advantage. The last attributes of dynamic capabilities, as described by Pavlou and El Sawy (2011), is coordinating capability. Coordinating capability can be described as the management and deployment of internal assets to manage the organizational change. Sensing capability can be described as a function of strategic exploration, while learning capability, integrating capability, and coordinating capability can be grouped under the exploitation of dynamic capabilities.

Leaders in several organizations have had difficulties in making a sound decision in a tough management environment. Pavlou and El Sawy (2011) described the purpose of dynamic capabilities as a process and method that will help the organization to modify, extend, and manage assets in the organization for appropriate reaction to a turbulent environment with the use of existing capabilities. Due to the challenges and ambiguity that surrounds the understanding of dynamic capabilities, leaders find it challenging to implement a capability that is dynamic without an in-depth knowledge of internal workings of the organization (Pavlou & El Sawy, 2011).

After the management of organizational assets, the next step for an organization is to scan the external environment and adjust resources for competitive advantage. Nooteboom (2010) explained exploration has a key strategic attribute of dynamic capabilities that will create sustainability for an organization. Firms need to have the ability to exploit the internal resources, as well as external opportunities, to form dynamic capabilities to attain the required competitive advantage for short and long-term sustainability (Nooteboom, 2010). There have been several researchers who have argued the long-time sustainability of an organization rooted in management's ability to explore emerging opportunities and exploit existing talent and competencies (Nooteboom, 2010; Jansen et al., 2009). The ability of an organization to explore opportunities and exploit internal assets is the centerpiece of dynamic capability that an organization can use for sustainment and competitive advantage. Project management is a field where dynamic capabilities are important due to the constant change that exists between stakeholders and external environmental factors. Based on the constant change in the field of project management, there is a need for leadership to structure organization assets for exploitation and exploration.

Situational Leadership Skills and Change Management

Bryman et al. (2011) described the need for change as an essential aspect of organization for competitive advantage. The organization influences some changes through external pressure. The external pressure can include external customers, politics, economy, and competitors external to the organization. The project management in an organization is challenged in managing shifts in priorities and delivery change cycles. When there is a sudden change that could be driven by the customer or other environmental influences, it is important for an organization to have the dynamic capability to exploit internal resources that will manage these types of change.

Exploitation of internal resources during change ensures that an organization will not have to hire outside experts or invest a significant amount of money to deal with a technological change during project execution (Lavie & Stettner & Tushman, 2010). Exploitation will help the organization to adequately allocate resources and align resources to meet the needs of project execution (Lavie et al., 2010). Organizations need to explore and discover new technologies to further the abilities of efficiently executing customer projects. Technology exploration will provide new ways to solve the problem through knowledge creation, which will yield long-term competitive advantage for organizations and will save operating costs (Farhad & Khairuddin & Roohangiz; 2011).

Transformational Leadership Skill

The popularity that transformational leadership has received reflects preliminary studies that have been conducted linking transformational leadership skills to organizational improvement. The attributes of transformational leadership are essential for project managers to influence and motivate their team to achieve deliverables and project objectives. Transformational leadership can be defined as the ability to create a significant identification and shared a vision with employees beyond rewarding activity completion (Nixon et al., 2012; McCleskey, 2014). Transformational leadership skill sets instill optimism and motivation to encourage team members to achieve a common goal.

Byman et al. (2011) explained transformational leadership as the method used to motivate and improve a follower's performance through a common commitment beyond an individual goal. McCleskey (2014) explained the correlation between transformational leadership skill set and management effectiveness. Transformational leadership goes beyond the motivation of followers and also seeks to develop leaders among the followers. What makes transformational leadership unique is the ability to implant a greater purpose into the mind of the follower, which will enable them to transcend and see beyond individual self-interest (McCleskey, 2014).

One of the key items that make transformational leadership unique is the ability to function beyond leader and follower transactions, as well as to accommodate the consideration of individuals in the group. The four main attributes of transformational leadership are intellectual simulation, individual consideration, inspirational motivation, and idealized influencing (McCleskey, 2014).

Idealized influence attributes of transformational leadership skill enable a leader to influence followers through a shared vision (Doody & Doody, 2012). Idealize influence can be categorized into two sections that include the ability of a leader to inspire followers by demonstrating specific behaviors, and how followers relate their desired attributes to the leader (McCleskey, 2014). Followers will tend to accept a leader who has similar ideas and attributes to what the follower desires. Similarities in ideas between a leader and a follow will create a common interest. McCleskey (2014) explained how the behavior of transformational leaders influences followers. Idealize influence is the process by which the leader and follower share a common vision through the influence and idea of the leader (Doody & Doody, 2012). Idealized influence skill enhances the ability of a project manager to influence the project team to accomplish project goals and focus on project priorities (Aga &Noorderhaven & Vallejo, 2016; Keegan & Hartog, 2004).

Individual consideration allows a leader to support followers by acting as a mentor to help them in achieving their goals (McCleskey, 2014). Leaders use individual consideration to provide a supportive environment for followers that equips followers in reaching their goals and ambitions (McCleskey, 2014). Individual consideration is an essential skill in the field of project management due to the ability to interact with the project team on a personal level.

Tse et al. (2013) conducted research that showed the effect of individual consideration on employee turnover in organizations. There are several studies that have been focused on understanding the relationship between employee turnover and transformational leadership. Turnover in organizations was high when there is little connection between leadership and the project team.

Successful leaders must *intellectually stimulate* their followers to get the best out of them. Intellectual simulation helps leaders to increase followers' intellectual abilities by challenging followers' assumptions and helping the followers to envision different approaches to solve problems (**McCleskey, 2014**). Intellectual stimulation from the leaders will improve the problem-solving skills of followers and their self-efficacy. Innovation among followers will increase when they operate in an environment where ideas are welcomed without criticism from the leader. How a leader intellectually stimulates followers is important to ensure that followers are not intimidated or timid. When there is a mutual interest in objectives or goals, followers were more accepting to receive intellectual stimulation from a leader. Project managers could use intellectual stimulation to develop learning agility in followers and aid improvement in continuous learning. It can be said that a project that exhibits a significant number of unknowns will require skills beyond planning and managing. There's a significant amount of innovation, problem-solving, and learning needed to mitigate and solve for project unknowns during the lifecycle of a project. Transformation leadership skill equips leaders with the ability to be innovative and motivate team members to be innovative.

The last aspect of transformation leadership skill is *inspiration motivation*. Transformational leaders contribute inspiration and optimism to every individual in the group. Inspirational motivation involves attributes that encourage with optimism and enthusiasm (McCleskey, 2014). One of the basic responsibilities of a leader is to motivate followers to accomplish desired goals. This type of motivation can be possible by utilizing behaviors that are inspirational to followers. Leaders are successful in motivating followers by creating an inspirational vision, installing similar identities, and portraying a confident vision (Grant, 2012).

Followers can be motivated when they believe there are similar ideas and core values between them and the leader. This similarity of core values and interests will eliminate the extrinsic aspect of the relationship and ensure that the relationship is more focused on intrinsic attributes. Individuals motivated inspirationally tend to be more successful and persevere due to the common goal and vision that are shared with the leader. Transformational leaders inspire their team by motivating them to aspire in meeting common goals. Transformational leadership skill creates the culture of motivating followers to operate beyond their interest and put the interest of the team first (Grant, 2012). There is an important link between motivation and personal interest that leaders need to understand. When followers shared a common interest in goals with the leader, there was a sense of purpose and motivation for the followers to contribute towards the goal. It will take a transformational event to change the culture of an individual from only thinking of self-interest to putting the interest of the team, group, organization, or society first. This type of thinking and mindset is challenging because most people naturally think of themselves first in many situations.

A leader needs to have essential transformational attributes to be successful in making this change and creating the culture in followers. Transformational leadership is effective, and the effect that it has in a group cannot be denied, but it takes leaders that understand these attributes and implement the attribute to be successful. Before an individual can be regarded as a transformation leader, there is a need for high level of competence in all four attributes, and the continuous development of these attributes is essential.

Transformational leadership is essential when it comes to innovation and problem-solving. Transformational leadership skill creates a system for an organization to work together as a cohesive team and share ideas among one another. This leadership methodology is critical for innovation in a work environment because it not only focuses on the interaction between a leader and a follower, but also emphasizes the dynamic of the team. It is easier for a group of people to solve a given problem by brainstorming ideas together and sharing knowledge that is beneficial to the goal of the organization.

This leadership theory creates a culture of team success rather than of individual success, which reduces the pressure of failure from individuals in the organization. Several companies today have been trying to create this culture in their organization. Organizations have worked on creating an open workspace environment to facilitate the collaboration of individuals within a team and increase their interactions. Teams that freely share ideas and knowledge tend to be more successful than teams that believe in individual accomplishments. It takes transformational leadership skill to create the process and culture in an organization that will encourage each person in the group to share ideas while putting followers' needs into consideration (Bryman et al., 2011).

Transformational leadership skill is essential for project managers to implement **change during project execution**. There is a strong correlation between transformational leadership and change. Change is an essential aspect of organization management due to the need of reinvention for competitive advantage. The change in transformational leadership skill is associated with a strategy to influence a group of people into a different paradigm of direction (Osula & Ng, 2014). There are several aspects that can cause change during the execution of a project, including competitive adjustment, economic atmosphere, and organization adjustment.

Based on the trend of the degree of change and risks associated with complex projects, it can be assumed that organizations will continue to change, which makes it essential to understand the appropriate methodology to manage change in the organization. Bryman et al. (2011) explained that transformational leadership is more efficient in change management. Transformational leadership skill will use the common interest of the group as a key platform of the change that is being introduced, which will make the whole team feel invested in the idea of change.

There is a sense of individual ownership that a transformational leadership skill will plant inside the followers to enable the followers to embrace the idea of change as their own. This type of leadership is beyond the basic contractual exchange between a leader and a follower to fulfill a purpose, and it incorporates the individual values of each member of the organization into the change system (Bryman et al., 2011). This change can happen by challenging individuals in the organization to see beyond their values and comfort zone and provide input on how they would like the change to be incorporated into the organization. The success of a change in an organization depends on how the change was implemented. The most effective way to implement change is by involving all stakeholders, which is an integral aspect of transformational leadership (Bryman et al., 2011). Transformational leadership skills and the usage of these attributes can contribute to successful project outcome. Organization and corporations have accomplished significant improvement in workforce retention, improvement in innovation, and employee satisfaction when project leaders utilize transformational leadership skill in their organization.

Relational Leadership Skill

While the concept of relational leadership is fairly new in leadership theory, it is one of the most important aspects of leadership in society. Relational leadership can be described as the process that enables leadership to grow through relationships to attain positive change (Uhl-Bien, 2006; Raffo, 2012). Relational leadership skill as a system that allows both the leader and followers to benefit from each other (Cunliffe & Eriksen, 2011). This leadership skill does not consider leadership as a leader and follower interaction, but as a process that fosters the growth of leadership in the society to attain important goals (Uhl-Bien, 2006; Raffo, 2012). Trust and integrity are essential aspects of this leadership methodology, if it is to be successful. There are five significant attributes of relational leadership skills that are essential for team building and could improve the strength of the project team, which are inclusiveness, being purposeful, empowering, process-oriented, and ethical (Raffo, 2012).

These attributes are important for leaders and project managers to meet a desired project outcome. Relational leadership skill uses inclusiveness to understand the diversity that exists with people and creates a relationship that accomplishes mutual goals with individual incorporation point of view (Fairhurst & Uhl-Bien, 2012; Hollander, 2009). The importance of inclusiveness of every member of a complex project team cannot be underestimated due to the need for solving these complex problems.

Relational leadership promotes the inclusion of every member of the group during decision-making without relying on the idea of an individual to create the idea or the vision (Hollander, 2009). This leadership skill creates confidence in team members to readily contribute to the project. Relational leadership skill empowers individuals in an organization by sharing responsibility and gives people a sense of ownership in the organization (Martin, Liao, & Campbell, 2013; Raffo, 2012). Project leaders with relational leadership skill help project team members to take an active role and personal responsibility in the leadership process and increase the improvement that every member will have in the leadership process (Raffo, 2012). Martin & Campbell (2013) researched the United Arab Emirates (UAE) and showed the importance of empowerment in an organization.

Relational leadership skill creates a sense of purpose and opportunity for every member of the group to commit to a common goal (Raffo, 2012). When every member of the team is committed to a common goal, the optimistic spirit within the group will significantly increase and potentially lead the participant to achieve goals that will make a significant difference. Project leaders with a relational leadership skill use process orientation to build the relationship in a group and establish the process of how the group was sustained to accomplish individual goals.

Process orientation can be described as the ability of followers and leaders to work together with synergy to accomplish positive change in the organization (Raffo, 2012). Relational leadership is regarded as one of the best ethical systems due to the ability to create standards that are driven by common values (Raffo, 2012). Ethics is integrated into relational leadership that allows individuals in the group to look beyond self-interest and contribute to one another's goals in attaining higher performance (Giessner & Quaquebeke, 2010).

A relational leadership system does not focus on a leader or follower, but instead focuses on a leadership system that interacts with people, keeping their interests and goals in mind. Relational leadership is centered on trust and communication between people in the community where they feel empowered in achieving goals. This leadership theory creates a purpose and a process where both leaders and followers can benefit from one another. Relational leadership explains that leadership does not necessarily have to be a top to bottom system and the key aspect of leadership is the relationship. This relationship starts with how individuals in the organization communicate with each other, the trust between individuals, and ethics. Leadership cannot be established without communication, ethics, and trust between leaders and followers, which is why relational leadership is an integral aspect of the leadership theory. Even though the idea of relational leadership is great, this theory is still relatively new, and there has not been enough research completed on the leadership theory. The lack of sufficient definition of the leadership theory could cause some misinterpretation on what the leadership theory stands for and how to sufficiently implement the leadership theory in the community.

Project Management

Spalek (2014) explained the influence of project management on enhancing successful project outcome, which is the reason why organizations are expanding their project management capabilities. Project management can be described as the application of tools, techniques, and knowledge of project activities that will facilitate and enhance the success of the project (PMBOK, 2013). The application of unique skills is needed in the completion of a project due to the complexity of managing a project. The practice of project management has expanded and is being utilized in several facilities and organizations to ensure projects meet success criteria (DuBois et al., 2015; Spalek, 2014; Handzic & Durmic, 2015).

Project management has become essential in the engineering industry due to the need to manage complexity and the ability to increase meaningful collaboration for goal attainment. There are significant issues in project management due to the increase in the complexity that is integrated into a project. Project management has been deemed the optimal approach to executing complex programs that were difficult to manage with a traditional method and still deliver innovations (Avots, 1969; Stoshikj et al., 2014; PMBOK, 2013).

The goal of a project manager is to ensure that the project management process is followed and to attain a successful project outcome. Leading a project to a successful outcome creates a challenge for project managers because most project managers are aligned to a matrix organization without direct reports, but they are still responsible for the outcome of the project (Gehring, 2007). PMBOK (2013) and Gehring (2007) described a matrix organization as a type of organization where project teams report directly to a functional manager instead of a project manager.

Project management entails the interaction of several cross-functional teams in the organization, which typically contributes to the complexity of the execution of project management. Due to the complexity and ambiguity of managing projects, organizations are relying on project management to reduce the duration of projects and significantly reduce costs while meeting the scope outlined by the stakeholders (Spalek, 2014).

PMBOK (2013) described five program management groups that are necessary and required to complete a project lifecycle, which is: initiating, planning, executing, monitoring, and controlling and closure. Planning and initiating are the early stages of project management that facilitate the creation of specific requirements and guidelines that help in meeting the deliverables of the project (PMBOK, 2013). Execution and controlling stages of the program are the phases that implement the requirements of the project. These are the phases that manage the risk and ensure that all defined requirements have been implemented to meet the expectations of the program.

The last management group in project management is the closure group. This is the group that ensures all requirements and guidelines have been met and the product or service has been successfully delivered to the appropriate stakeholder. A project can be closed when all requirements have been met or when the project has been terminated (PMBOK, 2013).

A project manager is typically assigned to lead the implementation of all phases of the project management lifecycle. Project managers are the strategic links of all the phases of the project management lifecycle and are typically responsible for ensuring that all phases of the program are completed to meet expected delivery of the project.

Project

A project can be defined as the achievement of a unique service or product through a set of activities or tasks (PMBOK, 2013; Stoshikj et al., 2014). What makes a project unique is the fact that it has a beginning and an end. Anca (2013) explained that a project is a set of activities that is guided through a set of prearranged plans to meet specific objectives for the organization. Handzic and Durmic (2015) further defined a project as a temporary and complex endeavor that produces services or goods to satisfy the expectation of stakeholders through completion within budget, on time, and meets expected specifications. Projects are interconnected with change, are more complex, and require a great deal of innovation (Murugesan 2012).

Spalek (2014) described three important basic attributes of a project to be budget, scope, and time. The project is completed when the strategic objectives have been accomplished, or if it has been terminated at the request of stakeholders (PMBOK, 2013). The outcome of a project can either be a service, product, or a specific result. A project can be executed at all levels of the organization to improve the existing business of that organization and implement a new process or product to improve the competitive advantage of the company.

Issues in Project Management

Due to the complexity surrounding the practice of project management, there are significant issues in project management that typically hinder a successful project outcome. Handzic and Durmic (2015) explained that approximately 70 percent of projects failed due to lack of on-time delivery, being over budget, or having an increase in scope. Cerpa and Verner (2009) described a report that was published in 2007 that identified 46 percent of projects that failed or did not meet the expectation of the stakeholders (Besteiro et al., n.d).

There are several project management courses on skills and methodology that are being taught in organizations, but research is still showing a high percentage of projects that are failing or which do not meet the expectation of the customer. Cerpa and Verner (2009) conducted a survey questionnaire on 235 projects and selected 70 projects that stakeholders considered failures. These failed projects were selected from various countries around the world including the United States, Australia, and Chile. The findings in the failure factors included an unpleasant experience by staff members, lack of reward and incentive for working long hours, an aggressive schedule that affected the motivation of the team, poor risk management, and mitigation process, just to name a few factors. These are issues that could be easily mitigated by effective, efficient, and well-developed leadership skills.

Lack of understanding of ownership is one of the significant issues in project management. Team members within the organization should understand their responsibilities and the risks of completing their activities. Lack of efficient communication and ownership results in lack of progress in the execution of projects. The lack of progress in the project will result in the delayed completion, which will contribute to the failure of the project. Project managers face a significant issue of motivating employees to fully perform and contribute to activities that will help a project to be successful. The lack of motivation and commitment is one of the main issues that cause projects to fail in the organization. Lack of motivation occurs due to employees not believing in the vision of the project, or because the incentive does not match the effort that they are putting towards the completion of the project.

Project Management and Complexity

The majority of technology-based projects are complex and difficult to manage due to the rise of expectations of stakeholders pushing the project team to perform. PMBOK (2013) described project management as the application of techniques, knowledge, and tools on projects to improve the successful outcome of a project. Brady and Davies (2104) explained the correlation of project failure with the inability of the organization to manage complexity. There is a significant interaction of multiple functional teams in project management during project execution. Complexity is the process of integrating a different number of independent variables that have a unique ideology of relations and interactions (Araujo & Franca, & Moura, n.d; Chroneer & Bergquist, 2012). The complexity level of a project can be judged on how well defined the goals are and the level of interdependencies between variables or components. Araujo et al. (n.d) and Chroneer and Bergquist (2012) further explained that the existence of uncertainty in a project due to lack of definition is one of the attributes that contribute to complexity in the project decision-making process. Brady and Davies (2014) explained that organization and technological complexity are the two sections of complexity that exist during project execution. Project leaders need to decide on selecting the right people who will form the project team to ensure talent selection fits the organization's culture.

Chroneer and Bergquist (2012) explained that project management involves planning, scheduling, and controlling activities that are necessary to complete a project, which further explains the importance of sound decision making.

Brady and Davies (2014) further explained the important role that complexity plays in the determination of the successful outcome of a large engineering project. The complex project experience of about 50 percent cost overrun and 100 percent overrun is not unusual for some projects (Brady & Davies, 2014). The existence of complexity in a project does not necessarily mean the project will fail, but there is a different set of leadership skills that are essential to achieving successful project outcome.

Kodukula (2011) explained that the application of complexity in project management is typically related to the management of virtual teams. Brady and Davies (2014) argued that complexity in project management is divided into dynamic and structural complexity. Complexity in project management does not always correlate to large projects, but to the management of teams within the project system. Complexity in project management is still generally ambiguous, and there is a lack of proper definition of its context (Chroneer & Bergquist, 2012).

De Souza Pinto et al. (n.d) further elaborated on the challenge of standardizing and accurately quantifying the level of complexity in a project. Organizations that execute complex programs have paid little attention to complexity, and there is a lack of awareness of the impact of contingency theory, systems analysis, and how they relate to complex projects.

One of the applications of complex systems in project management is the ability to manage a cross-functional team within the organization and create a self-organization methodology that will generate innovation during project implementation. Saynisch (2010) further explained the inability of traditional project management tools and processes to efficiently solve complex problems due to economics and advancement in technology. The challenge in the management of complex projects is the rationale behind the exploration of methodology to accomplish success when managing complex projects. There is a direct relationship between complexity theory and project management. Spalek (2014) and Handzic and Durmic (2015) described the increase in complexity of managing projects due to the existence of new technologies and cross-functional teams in the organization. Cerpa and Verner (2009) explained the trend of project failures due to lack of on-time delivery and going over budget due to complexity.

One of the contributing factors of the exponential failure rate of a project is due to consistent existent of complexity through the lifecycle of specific projects. The interaction and relationship of project management and complexity theory cannot be ignored. Randolf (2013) described the relationship between project and complexity as an essential aspect of project management for the professional to become more proficient. Depending on the context and organization that is executing a project, complexity can vary from one organization to another. Brady and Davies (2014) contextualized the three main contributing attributes of complexity in larger engineering projects as the organizational, environmental, and technical concepts. The technical aspects of large engineering complexity framework contain the ability to meet the tasks, goals, and scope. Organization complexity contains the ability to have enough resources to accomplish a specific project and the size of the project.

The environmental complexity includes the market environment, functional team location, and the perspective of stakeholders. Current literature in project management has elaborated on uncertainty and contingency framework of complexity in project management (Brady & Davis, 2014; Chroneer & Bergquist, 2012). Dynamics complexity can be described as changes in goals or specification in a project that could happen due to an internal or external environment. Complexity in project management can also be tied to uncertainty. Organizations tend to correlate uncertainty with complexity in project management due to the fear of the unknown. It is essential for the organization to have dynamic capabilities to respond to uncertainty during the lifecycle of a project. Boulton et al. (2015) further validated the fear of uncertainty in project management by defining complexity as emergent and episodic.

There are complexities in managing risks in a project. Project risk can be described as an uncertain condition or one that can negatively or positively affect the outcome of a project (Zivkovic, 2015). Thermahin (2013) explained how the importance of an organization to successfully deal with a project's complexity is integral to their success in today's competitive environment. The risk in a project is centered on uncertainty, which is what makes complexity one of the most important attributes to track in a project.

The uncertainty of risk management makes it challenging for the project team to understand how to effectively track and manage risks in projects. The existence of risks creates surprises for stakeholders through the lifecycle of the project. The impact of risk in a project ranges from financial performance market timing, technical feasibility, and ability to meet the strategic objective of the program.

There are ambiguities and uncertainties that are interconnected in a project, which makes the project complex to manage (Thermahin, 2013). Zivkovic (2015) explained multiple studies that have identified the correlation between project risk management and project success. There was an empirical study that was performed in China, according to Zivkovic (2015), that expands on the positive impact that risk management strategies have on a new product development project.

Leadership in Project Management

The effect of leadership on the success or failure of a project is the fundamental difference between project management and project leadership (Nixon et al., 2012).

Nixton et al. (2012) described project management as organizing and planning product activities through decision making for project effectiveness, while project leadership is guiding and motivating employees to attain challenging organizational goals and project objectives. The usage of the leadership skills by project managers is one of the determining factors in the outcome and success of a project. The ability of a leader to use and utilize leadership skills in a project is essential to enhancing the success rate of the project (Nixon & Harrington, & Parker, 2012). Transformational leadership skill is an essential skill that project managers can use to enhance the success of their projects.

Literature has shown that lack of motivation is one of the most significant reasons that a project does not meet the desired expectation. Cerpa and Verna's (2009) survey of failed projects showed lack of motivation from employees as one of the highest contributing factors for project failure. Project success requires a project manager with transformational leadership skill to inspirationally motivate employees to believe in the deliverables, to achieve the tasks, and to set an appropriate vision that employees can follow. Having transformational leadership skills enable a project manager to significantly motivate employees on milestones and deliverables that are needed to accomplish providing deliverables to stakeholders. Transformational leadership skills assist implementation of a shared vision with project teams and motivate the team to attain the vision without being motivated by reward (Nixon et al., 2012).

Engineering project managers have the challenges of managing complex programs, and the failures of these projects could affect the business environment of an organization. Project management is the process of planning, securing, managing, and organizing resources to achieve specific goals (Murugesan, 2012). Knowing the leadership style of a project manager will help organization leaders understand how a project manager will behave with team members and how he or she will lead the project (Clarke, 2012). Project motivation is an essential skill that project leaders need to master to ensure the project is running smoothly and successfully. Motivation is an essential skill that leaders need to have and knowing what motivates team members is essential for a project team (Murugesan 2012).

One of the reasons that projects fail is due to the lack of motivation by team members, and transformation leadership skill is centered on team motivation to attain a common goal. Rodriguez-Segura et al. (2016) described the classification of project failure or success as a multidimensional construct with dependency on several factors. Leadership that is successful convinces and influences employees to work together as a team, accomplish project objectives, and stimulates thinking processes to solve problems in a challenging environment (Nixon et al., 2012). Silva (2004) explained that one of the main characteristics of a leader is the ability to influence followers to achieve specific goals and visions.

Having the transformational leadership skill of idealizing influence will enable project managers to influence followers in accomplishing expected goals. Emotional intelligence as a skill that could significantly increase a positive project outcome. Nixon et al. (2012) described the correlation between different leadership styles and emotional intelligence, especially transformational leadership, which can improve the outcome of a project. An underdeveloped emotional intelligence will result in poor leadership, that will hinder a positive project outcome.

Need for Leadership Skills in Project Management

Leadership skills are essential in exploring, motivating, and setting vision (Nixon et al. 2012). One of the most common questions in leadership theory is if and how leadership can be developed. Literature has proven that leadership skills can be developed and efficiently used in an organization. Some of the issues associated with a project are the ability to gain commitment from the project team and to motivate project partners (Clark, 2012). It is imperative for leaders to implement leadership development programs for project managers based on the importance and impact of these leadership skills in project management. The effect of leadership on the success or failure of a project is the fundamental difference between project management and project leadership (Nixon et al., 2012). Nixon et al. (2012) described project management as organizing and planning product activities through decision making for project effectiveness, while project leadership is guiding and motivating employees to attain challenging organizational goals and project objectives. Transformational leadership skill is an essential skill that project managers can use to enhance the success of their project. It will take a project manager with a transformational leadership skill to inspirationally motivate employees to believe in the deliverables, to achieve the tasks, and to set an appropriate vision that employees can follow.

Having transformational leadership skills will enable a project manager to significantly motivate employees on milestones and deliverables that are needed to provide deliverables to stakeholders. Transformational leadership skills will implement a shared vision with project teams and motivate the team to attain the vision without being motivated by reward (Nixon et al., 2012). One of the reasons that projects fail is due to the lack of motivation by team members, and transformation leadership skill is centered on team motivation to attain a common goal. Leadership that is successful convinces and influences employees to work together as a team, accomplish project objectives, and stimulates thinking processes to solve problems in a challenging environment (Nixon et al., 2012). Silva (2004) explained that one of the main characters of a leader is to influence followers to achieve specific goals and vision.

Having the transformational leadership skill of idealizing influence will enable project managers to influence followers in accomplishing expected goals. Emotional intelligence is a skill that could significantly increase a positive project outcome. Nixon et al. (2012) described the correlation between different leadership styles and emotional intelligence, especially transformational leadership, which can improve the outcome of a project. It can be said that an under developed emotional intelligence will result in poor leadership, that will hinder a positive project outcome.

The ability to articulate strategic vision and deliverables, the ability to influence colleagues to believe in project goals, and the ability to motivate team members to achieve these goals are the three essential attributes that can significantly contribute to project success. Project management has helped in providing insight on how a project can be managed. Despite the utilization of project management skills, it can be said that most projects are still unsuccessful. It's important to understand project characteristics that enhance project success and the exercise of leadership by project managers is one of the key characteristics (Muller et al., 2010). The social capability of a leader is one of the essential aspects of leadership traits for project managers. Social capabilities enhance the networking skill of project leaders and the maintenance of lasting relationships. The combination of a leader's ability and willingness to lead are elements that should sought when selecting a program manager (Strang, 2007).

There is a need to understand how leaders can lead across boundaries and drive results in the context that each party has different values, goals, and expectations. Modern projects have complexity that requires project managers to have strong leadership skills (Miller & Balaputia, & Sesay, 2015). Managing these complicated projects across external boundaries adds to the challenges of project managers to drive successful outcomes in a collaborative situation. The training and development of collaborative leadership will help project managers have the skill set that can be used to lead across boundaries and get expected results.

Successful Project Outcome

The term "successful project" is often subjective and based on what the stakeholders of the project highlight as the requirements of success (Besteiro et al., n.d). Finding the right performance measures is essential to effectively understand how to determine the success factor of a project. The traditional approach to the attributes that determine a successful project is cost, time, and budget (Besteiro et al., n.d; Spalek, 2014; Gemunden, 2015).

These three attributes are also known as the golden triangle of success criteria in project management (Spalek, 2014). Gemunden (2015) further explained that there are three other attributes that should be put into consideration in the definition of project success. Nixon et al. (2012) described project management as budget, schedule, termination efficiency, functionality, and client satisfaction as important attributes that determine project success. The iron triangle (cost, scope, and schedule) are important, but understanding stakeholders' value is also a key aspect of successful project outcome. Organizations are driven to ensure projects are completed on time, within budget, and meet the expected scope that was initially identified by stakeholders. One of the most important actions that determine the success factor of a project is the role that a project manager plays as a leader during a project (Muller et al., 2010). Part of the responsibility of a program manager is to deliver expected project outcomes for the organization, which can be optimized by influencing the project team to focus on the common goal (Muller et al., 2010).

Leadership development for project managers

It is imperative for leaders to implement leadership development programs for project managers based on the importance and impact of implementing leadership skills in project management. The ability to articulate strategic vision and deliverables, influence colleagues to believe in project goals, and motivate team members to achieve these goals are the three essential attributes that can significantly contribute to project success. Developing the ability of project managers to have these leadership skills will facilitate completion of projects and meeting the objective. Project managers can develop an emotional intelligence skill set by improving self-awareness and having the patience to understand others' emotions. There are self-awareness tools like Emotional Quotient Inventory (EQ-I) that project managers can use to understand weaknesses, strengths, and areas to develop emotional intelligence.

Summary

This chapter has identified the role and impact of leadership skills in project management. It explained the important role that leadership skills play in project management and how the absence or presence of those skills can influence the outcome of a project. There have been several research studies on project management and leadership, but there is a significant gap in how these two attributes integrate with each other for a successful project outcome. Project management plans and strategically organizes project activities, while leadership motivates and influences project teams to achieve and accomplish project deliverables. Leadership skills are an essential tool that project managers can use to influence project outcome.

Chapter III

METHODOLOGY

Introduction

As stated in Chapter 1, the purpose of this study is to explore the leadership skills in project managers and to understand how they contribute to successful project outcomes in the aerospace and defense industry. Previously, there have been some successful projects and others that have not been successful (Besteiro et al., 2015; Nixon et al, 2012; Blaskovics, 2016). Multiple studies have described the importance of leadership skills in the field of project management (Anca, 2014; DuBois et al., 2015; Nixon et al, 2012). The importance of leadership skills in project management in the aerospace industry is still a fairly new concept and there is limited research on how leadership skills can enhance the ability of project managers in this industry. This study explored the projects that are successful and attempted to understand why they are successful. Achieving success in the aerospace industry is essential due to the cost that is associated with these projects.

This qualitative multiple case study further explored how project managers use leadership skills and the factors that enhance their ability to demonstrate leadership traits and behavior in the aerospace and defense industry. This study provided insight on how project managers use leadership skills in their successful projects and revealed methods used by project managers to enable successful completion of selected projects. Current literature discusses the importance of leadership in the field of project management, but little definitive information exists as to the importance of leadership as used in the aerospace and defense industry. In addition to the determination of utilization of leadership skills by project managers, an exploration of project success criteria was conducted to understand how project managers recognize project success.

The research methodology was designed in order to address the research questions listed in Chapter 1. The research questions that were presented are:

1. What are the leadership skills, as examined by the Leadership Development Questionnaire (LDQ) in project management that may contribute to successful project outcomes in the aerospace and defense industry?

2. How does the practice of leadership by project managers contribute to successful project outcomes in the aerospace and defense industry?

The results from participant interviews generated new knowledge on leadership skills which project managers can later utilize in the aerospace and defense industry.

The remainder of Chapter III is an overview of research design and the structure of this study, including sampling, and population.

Research Design

A qualitative multiple case study was used for this research study due to the ability to examine phenomenon within its context (Guest & Namey & Mitchell, 2013). Four cases were examined in this research design to explore the context in which project managers utilize leadership skills in their organization. The primary purpose of the multiple case study is to understand the types of leadership skills that successful project managers use in their organizations. The premise of utilizing a case study for this research study is to understand what makes these project managers successful in regard to their leadership skills. A multiple case study allowed for the extraction of leadership skills and traits from the different environments of project managers.

The purpose of using a multiple case study is that it provides the ability to analyze differences between multiple cases with the aim of replicating the findings between all the cases (Baxter & Jack, 2008). In the past, there have been criticisms of using a single case study because that only addresses and analyzes a single situation (Yin, 2008).

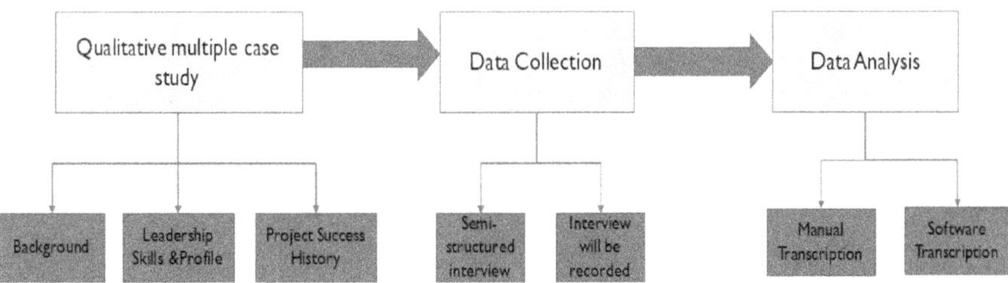

Figure 4 Research Method Process

To fulfill the purpose of this research study, a multiple case study was used with in depth phenomenological interviews as the instrument to collect data. Phenomenology focuses on individuals and their experiences. Phenomenology uses techniques such as open-ended questions and conversation enquiry to explore the perspective of participants for a given phenomenon (Bazeley, 2013). The interview is deemed to be the optimal method for a multiple case study due to the ability to acquire in-depth information and to also ask follow-up questions for clarification on necessary context. Historical project documentation was collected before the interview and used during the interview process to enhance the ability of project managers to discuss the success of their project and to understand how their leadership skills enhance the success of their projects.

The interview questions were divided into three categories: background of participants, leadership skills, and project success criteria. The interview questions are developed by the researcher based on the Leadership Development Questionnaire instrument by Dulewics and Higgs (2005) and a project success criteria tool developed by

Muller and Tuner's (2007).

Background of Participants: Questions in this section assessed the experience

level of project managers in the aerospace and defense industry and the experience level

in managing engineering and technology projects.

Leadership Skills and Profiles: Questions regarding leadership traits and styles of

selected project managers were used to understand the leadership characteristics that

enhance the project manager's ability to lead his/her team to successful project outcomes.

The leadership interview questions were developed within the context of the Leadership

Development Questionnaire (LDQ) instrument as described by Dulewics and Higgs

(2005). This leadership assessment tool is often used in the examination of leadership

skills, especially in the field of project management (Muller & Turner, 2010). LDQ was

used to profile emotional competence, managerial effectiveness, and intellectual

capabilities (EQ, MQ, and IQ) of project manager participants with successful project

outcomes. The interview questions were derived from 15 leadership competencies

developed by Muller and Turner (2010) and was inspired by three leadership styles:

Emotional (EQ), managerial (MQ), and Intellectual (IQ) as described by Dulewics &

Higgs (2005).

Leadership Styles	Competencies	Description
Intellectual (IQ)	Critical Analysis and Judgment	A critical faculty that probes the facts, identifies advantages and disadvantages, and discerns the shortcomings of ideas and proposals. Makes sound judgments and decisions based on reasonable assumptions and factual information, aware of the impact of any assumptions made
	Vision and Imagination	Imaginative and innovative in all aspects of one's work. Establishes sound priorities for future work. A clear vision of

Leadership Styles	Competencies	Description
		the future direction of the organization to meet business imperatives. Foresees the impact of changes on one's vision that reflects implementation issues and business realities.
	Strategic Perspective	Sees the wider issues and broader implications. Explores a wide range of relationships, balances short- and long-term considerations. Sensitive to the impact of one's actions and decisions across the organization. Identifies opportunities and threats. Sensitive to stakeholders' needs and the implications of external factors on decisions and actions.
Managerial (MQ)	Engaging Communication	Plans, organizes all resources, and coordinates them efficiently and effectively. Establishes clear objectives. Converts long-term goals into action plans. Monitors and evaluates staff's work regularly and effectively; gives sensitive, honest feedback.
	Managing Resources	A lively and enthusiastic communicator engages others and wins support. Communicates instructions and vision to the staff. Communications are tailored to the audience's interests and focused. Communication style inspires staff and audiences, conveys approachability and accessibility.
	Empowering	Gives staff autonomy, encourages them to take on personally challenging or demanding tasks. Encourages them to solve problems, produce innovative ideas and proposals and develop their vision and a broader vision. Encourages a critical faculty and a broad perspective, and encourages the challenging of existing practices, assumptions, and policies.
	Developing	Believes others have the potential to take on ever more-demanding tasks and roles, encourages them to do so. Ensures direct reports have adequate support. Develops their competencies, and invests time and effort in coaching them, so they contribute effectively and develop themselves. Identifies new tasks and roles to develop others. Believes that critical feedback and challenge are important.
	Achieving	Willing to make decisions involving significant risk to gain an advantage. Decisions are based on core business issues and their likely impact on success. Selects and exploits activities that result in the greatest benefits to the organization and its performance. Unwavering determination to achieve objectives and implement decisions.

Leadership Styles	Competencies	Description
Emotional (EQ)	Self-awareness	Awareness of one's feelings and the capability to recognize and manage these feelings in a way that one feels that one can control. A degree of self-belief in one's capability to manage one's emotions and to control their impact in a work environment.
	Emotional Resilience	Performs consistently in a range of situations under pressure and adapts behavior appropriately. Balances the needs of the situation and task with the needs and concerns of the individuals involved. Retains focus on a course of action or need for results in the face of personal challenge or criticism.
	Motivation	Arrives at clear decisions and drives their implementation when presented with incomplete or ambiguous information using both rational and "emotional" or intuitive perceptions of key issues and implications.
	Sensitivity	Is aware of, and takes in to account, the needs and perceptions of others in arriving at decisions and proposing solutions to problems and challenges. Builds from this awareness and achieves the commitment of others to decisions and action. A willingness to keep open one's thoughts on possible solutions to problems and to actively listen to, and reflect on, the reactions and inputs from others.
	Influence	Persuades others to change views based on an understanding of their position and a recognition of the need to listen to this perspective and provide a rationale for change.
	Intuitiveness	Drive and energy to achieve clear results and make an impact. Balances short- and long-term goals with a capability to pursue demanding goals in the face of rejection or questioning.
	Conscientiousness	Displays clear commitment to a course of action in the face of challenge and to match "words and deeds" in encouraging others to support the chosen direction. Shows personal commitment to pursuing an ethical solution to a difficult business issue or problem.

Table 1 Muller & Turner Leadership Styles and Competencies

The competencies and styles show the effect of leadership on the successful

outcome of a project by exploring key leadership concepts such as emotional intelligence

(Trejo, 2016; Day, Harrison, & Halpin, 2008). The interview questions were generated

and influenced by the criteria in Table 1. The interview results were used to match the

elements of the criteria in Table 1. During the analysis of the interview data, the

researcher looked for themes and keywords that are reflected in Muller and Turner

Leadership Styles and Competencies described in Table1.

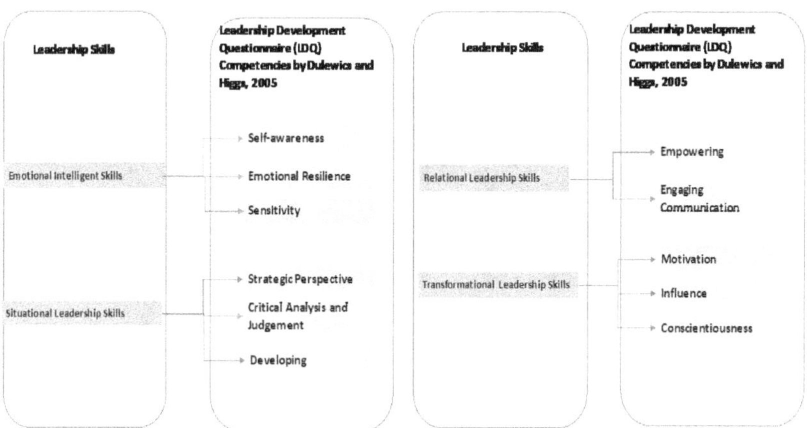

Figure 5 Matrix of Leadership Skills and LDQ

LDQ by Dulewics and Higgs (2005) was used to inform the interview questions

to assess essential leadership skills that enhance successful project outcomes. As

discussed in earlier chapters, understanding the context and the application of situational

intelligence, emotional intelligence, transformational skills, and relational skills could be

an essential tool that project leaders could use to enhance successful project outcome

(McCleskey, 2014; Cerpa &Verna, 2009; Nixon et al., 2012). Figure 5 shows the matrix

of leadership skills that were explored in this research study and how they are mapped to

the leadership competency assessment tool developed by Dulewics and Higgs (2005).

Figure 5 explains how the LDQ instrument was used to measure and explore leadership skills of successful project managers.

Project Success Criteria: Muller and Tuner's (2007) project success criteria tool was used to develop the interview questions related to the success of the project from the viewpoint of the project managers. The project success criteria developed by Muller and Tuner (2007) were used to determine the success and the satisfaction of the project as shown in Figure 5.

Figure 6 Project Success Criteria by Muller and Tuner (2007)

Methodology Selected

A qualitative multiple-case study was used to conduct this research due to the nature of the study and the research problem. Qualitative research enhances the ability to further explore the reality of people by interpreting, analyzing, and describing the context of the environment that they live in and how they think about themselves (Erlingsson & Brysiewics 2013; Bazeley 2013; Guest & Namey & Mitchell, 2013). Qualitative methodology explores the ability of individuals to construct their realities and is open to the idea of multiple truth. A qualitative method was chosen because it presents the ability to ask open-ended questions and can then be seamlessly integrated into the research study as described by Bazeley (2013). Qualitative research provides the means to explore the world of aerospace project managers and share insight of their leadership skills. Qualitative methodology is appropriate for this research study due to the rigor of in-depth questions that were asked about leadership while completing an aerospace and defense project. Qualitative methodology would allow close exploration about multiple open-ended questions of the practice of leadership by project managers.

This research methodology aligns with the exploration of understanding the leadership skills that enhance project managers' likelihood of being successful. The subjectivity that is inherent in qualitative methodology is essential in the study of leadership skills exploration in the context of the leadership and how it contributes to successful project outcome, which is why phenomenology was chosen to attain and understand the subjectivity of the candidate. The ability to understand the diversity and variation of life experiences of each participant is essential when conducting an explorative study in leadership traits and skills. Bazeley (2013) explained that qualitative methodology helps the researcher to focus on the quality of the data that is being retrieved rather than the quantity of it.

The quantitative research method is based on measuring the relationship between variables, which is deemed too restrictive for the exploration of leadership skills in project managers. Quantitative research is based on concluding numeric values with multiple participants of similar variables, which could not provide the depth of contextual meaning and relationship to what triggered the usage of leadership skills in the participants' day to day activities. The acquisition of statistical numerical data would not be enough to have an in-depth understanding of the contextual leadership culture of project managers.

Population and Samplings

The project managers selected for this multiple case study met selection criteria stated in Figure 6 to ensure that they have relevant project management experience. Participants selected for the multiple case study would have completed successful projects in the aerospace and defense industry, based on definition and criteria for project success by Muller and Turner (2007). These populations were selected due to the essential and important role that project managers play in completing a technology project in the aerospace and defense industry.

The criteria for the success of a project varies from project to project and according to the expectations of the project sponsors (Muller & Turner, 2007); however, for the purpose of this research study, successful project outcome was examined based on Muller and Turner's (2007) ten attributes that determine successful project outcome, including: overall project success, meeting user requirements, meeting project purpose, reoccurring business, customer satisfaction, end-user satisfaction, stakeholder's satisfaction, supplier satisfaction, team satisfaction, and self-defined success criteria. Figure 5 was provided to employers to fill out and confirm that the candidate has met the criteria for successful project outcome according to Muller and Turner's (2007) successful project outcome instrument.

The project managers selected had strong recommendations from their employers with the confirmation that they've met the successful project outcome criteria as shown in Figure 5, which shows that they have completed a project with successful outcomes. Selecting project managers who have completed a project is important because the essence of the research is to explore and understand leadership skills of successful project outcome. There was a total of four project managers selected for this research study based on the need to have in depth data that were analyzed to gain deeper understanding of the inquiry, which is a necessity, according to Bernard (2013). For the four cases that were studied, each program manager provided his/her self-assessment of the leadership skills and discussed the perception of project success through the interview questions that were asked.

Samples of project managers were selected from four states: Iowa, Illinois, Connecticut, and Oklahoma. These four states were selected due to the strong presence of aerospace and defense companies which enhanced the ability to get the required samples for the research. Program managers were selected from companies located within the four chosen states. The project managers were chosen from engineering and technology departments within an aerospace and defense company. The decision to sample from an engineering and technology department was made due to the complexity of managing a technology project within the aerospace and defense industry.

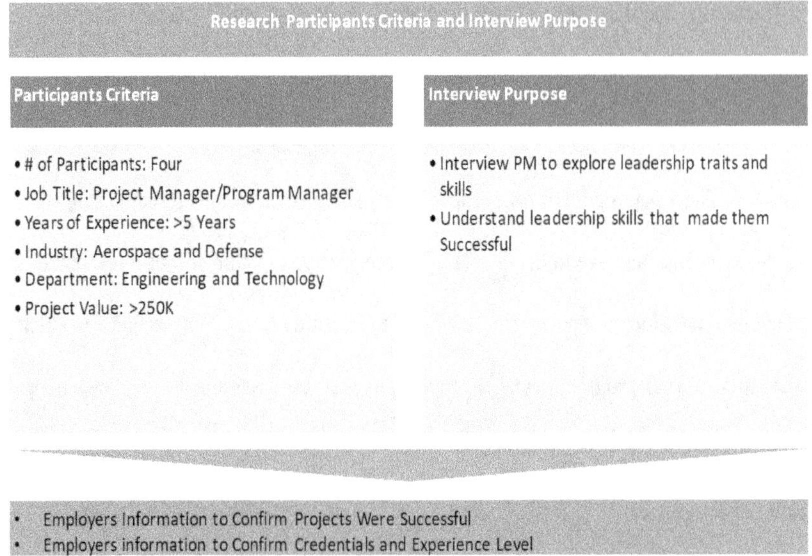

Figure 7 Research Participant Criteria

The four cases that were used for this research study were obtained based on the criteria described in Figure 6. The project managers who participated in this study were required to have more than five years of project management experience and have successfully managed a project with a value of more than 250 thousand dollars.

Process of Contacting Participants

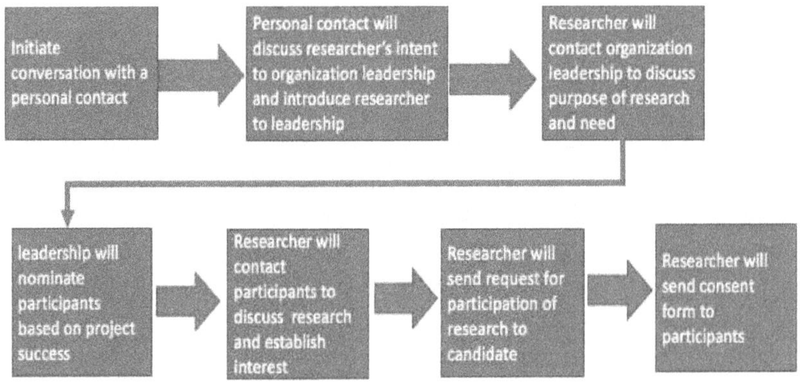

Figure 8 Participants Contact Process

Figure 8 shows the processes that were used to contact participants who were involved in the research study. The organization leadership or direct supervisor of the research participants confirmed that these participants met the criteria established by the researcher.

Data Collection

The leadership skills were explored with participants' understanding of the context in which these skills are utilized, what prompts the utilization of these skills, and their perception of what a successful project outcome is. A semi-structured interview was used to gain further understanding of the leadership skills and how selected project managers practice leadership to enhance successful project outcomes in their organization. The methodology used to contact participants was through prior professional networks that the researcher had already established.

The researcher has colleagues in targeted organizations that helped to recommend a candidate who would participate in the research study. The criteria of participants needed for the research was emailed to colleagues in these organizations and through their help the information was circulated to department heads who helped to confirm that research participants met requirements to participate in the research study. Requests to participate in the research study were distributed to 10 participants with the goal of selecting four candidates to participate in the study. Ten participates were selected for the initial request to ensure that there would still be enough participants in the study even if some potential candidates refused to participate.

There were two levels of informed consent provided to participants. The first consent form was sent through email to request their participation and to describe the objective of the research. The second informed consent forms were provided to participants prior to the interview in conjunction with IRB information and documentation. The interviews with participants were recorded to ensure the researcher was able to transcribe interview data and arrange that data in themes after the completion of the interview. Research participants were made aware that the interview was recorded and the researcher sought the approval of participants before taping the interview.

Procedures Followed

Interview Questions

There are three sets of interview questions used to collect valuable information from participants to support the research questions. Group one was developed to understand participants' background, professional qualifications, and academic background. Group two interview questions were developed to understand self-perceived assessment of participants' understanding of successful project outcome. Group three interview questions explored the leadership skills of the participants. Definitions of leadership competencies were provided participants to ensure consistency of data (self-assessment of specific skills rather than inadvertently assessing how they interpret or define the leadership terms) rather than their own interpretation.

Group 1 – Background Information

- Describe your professional experience.

- Describe your academic background.

- Describe your experience in managing engineering projects.

  o Describe your experience in managing aerospace & defense projects.

  o How many years of experience do you have managing these projects?

Group 2: Leadership Skills and Traits (Questions inspired and generated from Dulewics and Higgs, 2005)

- If "critical analysis and judgement" means the identification of advantages/disadvantages of ideas and making sound judgement based on reasonable assumption, then describe an example of a situation where you used critical analysis and judgement during the course of a project (Situational leadership skills)

  - What was the situation?

  - What was the impact on project members?

  - What was the outcome?

- If "strategic perspective" is the ability to understand the holistic implication of an issue, describe a situation where you used strategic perspective to impact the outcome of a problem during the course of a project (Situational leadership skills).

- If "empower" means the process of encouraging employees to make independent decisions, describe an example of a situation that you empowered your project team to make an innovative decision to solve a complex problem (Relational leadership skills).

  - What was the outcome?

- If "self-awareness" means recognizing and managing one's emotions and recognizing other's feelings, describe an example of a situation where you demonstrated self-awareness during the course of a project (Emotional leadership skills).

- If "emotional resilience" is the ability to remain focused under pressure, describe a situation where you demonstrated emotional resilience during the course of a project (Emotional leadership skills.
    - What was the outcome and the impact that it had on the project and project team?
- Describe a situation when you motivated your team to focus on project goals and project outcome (Transformational leadership skills).
- Describe a situation when you influenced your project leadership to change their position based on their current understanding (Transformational leadership skills).
    - What was the situation?
    - What was the outcome?
- Describe a situation when you developed one or more of your team members to solve a complicated problem during the course of the project (Situational leadership skills).
- If "conscientiousness" means staying committed to an action and encouraging others in a challenging situation, describe a situation where you showed conscientiousness during the course of a project (Transformational leadership skills).
    - Why did you need to do show conscientiousness?
    - What was the impact on the project team and other stakeholders?
    - What was the outcome of the project?

- If "sensitivity" means having awareness of others' needs and perceptions, explain a situation where you showed sensitivity to team members' feelings before proposing a solution to a problem (Emotional leadership skills).

- Describe a situation when you successfully engaged in communication with your project team members to clearly establish project goals and avenues for performance feedback (Relational leadership skills).

Group 3: Successful Project Outcome (Questions Generated from Muller and Tuner, 2007)

- What is the name of the project that you were discussing today?

- What is the summary, purpose, and the objective of the project that you were discussing today?

- Do the project specifics described today represent the type of projects that you usually work on?

- Do you believe that the project under discussion was successful?

  - What is your definition of project success?

  - Describe why you believe the project was successful.

- Describe how you believe the project met the intended goal and purpose. Explain how and why.

- Do you believe the project met the expectations of relevant stakeholders associated with the project?

  - How did the project meet the customer expectation?

  - How did the project meet the organization's expectation?

  - How did the project meet the project team's expectation?

- After the completion of the project, was there other follow-up business that was acquired from the customer?

Ethical Concerns

Participants were assured that their confidentiality will be kept intact after the study and that there will not be linkage to them through this research. The names and the organization of the participants will not be revealed in the research. The only person who will have access to participants' information was the researcher. The researcher used a unique identifier for each participant to protect his or her identity (for example, P01, P02, P03, and P04). Data from participants was kept safe in the researcher's laptop computer, which is secured by a password. The unique identifier was the method of identification of research participant and was created by the researcher

Data Analysis

After the completion of the interview process, five steps were taken to analyze the data gathered from participants. The interview was transcribed within three days after conducting the interview. The transcribing of the interview data was primarily executed manually by taking notes during the interview process. Transcription software was used as the secondary source to transcribe the audio interview to text. After receiving acknowledgement from participants, the researcher reviewed the transcribed data and took notes to identify themes in relation to the research question. The interview data was coded as means of identifying, sorting, and purposefully managing interview data as described by Bazeley (2013). Transcribed data was arranged to align with the research questions introduced in Chapter I.

The transcribed interview data was grouped into three categories for organization and theme management: 1) participants' background and geography information; 2) project outcomes; and 3) leadership skills. The first category included participants' information including academic background, geographic location, and relevant project management experience. The second category has information associated with project outcomes, and the third category has information on leadership skills which were used during the execution of this project. Direct quotations from participants were used to solidify and group interview data into appropriate categories. Leadership skills were characterized as one of four items: Emotional Intelligence, transformational skills, relational skills, and situational skills. Themes and threads were recorded from the interview questions and arranged in the four-leadership skills section for all participants.

Reliability and Validity

Reliability and validity are essential elements in a qualitative study to ensure the credibility of the research. Validity can be described as the level of accuracy to which the account represents participants' reality of the phenomenon and the phenomenon's credibility (Creswell, 2000). Qualitative research employs several techniques for validation including peer reviews, triangulation, and member checking (Creswell, 2000). For the purpose of this research study, triangulation was used as a validation methodology after the collection of data. Triangulation can be described as a validity tool that converges among multiple tools to form themes and categories of the research study (Creswell, 2000). Definitions of terms were provided with interview questions to ensure consistency of the meaning of interview questions. This ensured reliability on data retrieved from participants through the interview questions. Interview transcripts was also thoroughly reviewed to ensure that they are free of transcripts errors.

There were three dimensions of validity that were used. The first validity dimension was successful project outcome documentation that was provided to the employers of the project managers to show that the project they managed was successful. This documentation showed how their projects were completed on time and met the expectation of key stakeholders. The second dimension of validity was through the data that was collected during the interview and was distributed to participants to review the accuracy of the information after the interview (member checking). Lastly, the third validation criteria were through literature review and the ten characteristics of successful project outcomes as laid out by Muller and Tuner (2007). The results from the interview questions were cross-checked with the Muller and Turner's successful project outcome criteria. These three dimensions provided appropriate reliability and validity of the research data that were gathered. The objective of the transcribed data was to show themes between the examined data and to then establish a relationship to the research question.

There are two limitations that were associated with this research study. The first limitation was the number of participants. Even though there were enough participants to gather the information needed to drive the conclusions for the research, a larger sample size could also enhance further data collection. The second limitation of the research is the conduction of the research interview through virtual technology. There could be a limitation with conducting a virtual interview due the existence of body language that could be missed; however, the data that was gathered from the participants virtually was

compelling for the research.

Chapter IV

DATA ANALYSIS

Introduction

The purpose of this multiple case study is to explore the leadership skills in project managers and to understand how these leadership skills contribute to successful project outcomes in the aerospace and defense industry. This research study explored the leadership skills of successful project managers through a qualitative case study to understand how leadership skills were used to accomplish successful project outcomes. This research study detailed the specific leadership skills that these successful project managers used and how the use of these skills enhanced the success of the overall project.

The study design consisted of conducting a semi-structured interview with four successful program managers with a record of accomplishment in managing projects to successful outcomes in the past five years. Based on the criteria described in Chapter 3, four program managers were selected out of nine program managers who were invited to participate in the study. Three of the nine invited participants declined to participate in the study, while two did not have the time to help with the research. The remaining four agreed to participate in the research study. The interview questions further explored each participant's perception of how successfully they managed projects to completion and the type of leadership traits they displayed during the course of the project. Supporting documentation was received from the leadership and direct supervisor of the participants to substantiate project success history.

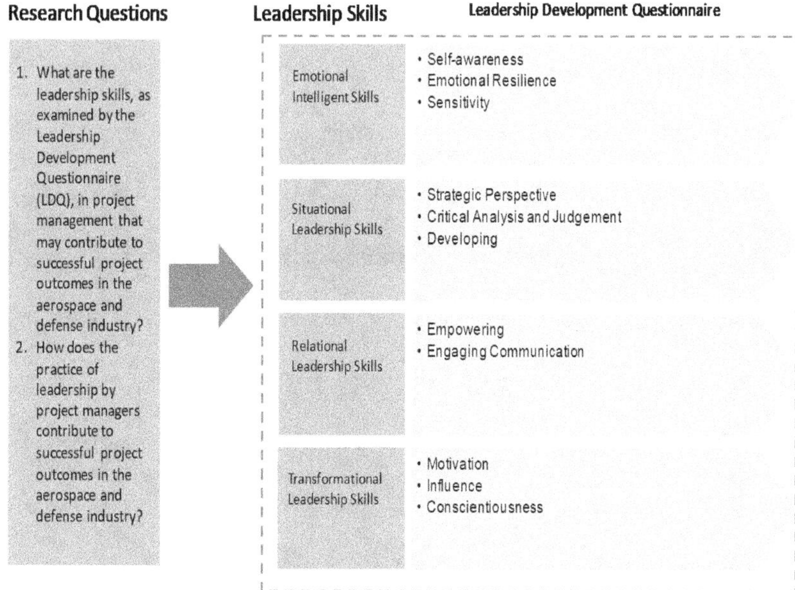

Figure 9 Interview Questions Construct

The research questions discussed in Chapter 1 asked how leadership skills contribute to successful project outcome by program managers in the aerospace and defense industry. The research questions were used to frame the leadership skills constructs that were explored with participants during the interview process as shown in Figure 9. The research questions are:

1. What are the leadership skills, as examined by the Leadership Development Questionnaire (LDQ), in project management that may contribute to successful project outcomes in the aerospace and defense industry?

2. How does the practice of leadership by project managers contribute to successful project outcomes in the aerospace and defense industry?

The four leadership skills constructs that were explored are emotional intelligent skills, situational leadership skills, relational leadership skills, and transformational leadership skills. Interview questions were developed from these four leadership constructs using Muller and Turner's (2010) Leadership Development Questionnaire to explore how participants used leadership skills during the course of their project. The interview questions were designed to answer the research questions that were discussed in Chapter 1. The program managers that participated in this study were involved in managing complex programs, dealt with internal/external pressure, and were successful in using leadership skills to achieve successful project outcomes.

Figure 10 shows the most frequently used words by the four participants who participated in this research. NVIVO was used to identify these frequently used words and is represented in the picture below. The world map in Figure 10 shows "project", "program", and "customer" as the most frequently used words by the participants and the leadership is a supportive attribute associated with these three words. Literature reviews further confirmed that leadership skills are essential for a project to have a successful outcome.

Figure 10: Top Frequency Word Used

Three categories of data were gathered during the interview process. The first category of data is the participants' demographics including background/experience, span of responsibilities, and years of experience in managing aerospace and defense projects. The second group of data is the perception of leadership skills used during the project execution to achieve successful project outcome. The third group of data is their perception of the candidate on the outcome of the projects that they have managed. During the discussion of the findings for the cases used in this study, participants were given the code names of P01, P02, P03, and P04 to protect identities.

Participants Background

Case #	Participants'	Years of Professional experience	Years of PM Experience	Undergraduate Degree	Graduate Degree	Position Title	Value of program Managed	Project Team	Project Duration
Case 1	P01	36	20	Nuclear Engineering	Masters in Mechanical Engineering	Program Manager	$10-150M	50-100	2-6 Years
Case 2	P02	15	10	Electrical Engineering	MBA	Program Manager	~$15M	15-25	2-5 years
Case 3	P03	21	11	Electrical Engineering	MBA & Masters in Electrical Engineering	Program Manager	$2-150M	25-80	1-5 years
Case 4	P04	16	10	Electrical Engineering	MBA	Program Manager	$5-149M	~120	2-5 years

Figure 11 Participants' Demographic Data

All participants selected for this study have college degrees in engineering, which is expected based on the industry that the study is associated with. Three out of the four participants have a bachelor's degree in electrical engineering, while the fourth participant has a bachelor's degree in nuclear engineering. All participants have master's degrees either in business administration or engineering. Three out of four participants have master's degrees in business administration and two have master's degrees in engineering (mechanical and electrical engineering).

All participants started their careers as engineers and progressed through promotion to program management. P03 and P04 have prior experience in the military with the knowledge of operating business in the defense sector. P01 has about sixteen years in engineering and twenty years in program management. P01, P02, and P04 established interests in going into program management and took roles that would prepare them for program management roles. P03 was the only participant who did not aspire to become a program manager, but was persuaded to take the role. P03 was encouraged to take a program management role due to the potential that was demonstrated. P03 summarized the initial response when offered the opportunity to become a program manager as follows: "There was a programs manager who's one up above me. He recognized some skills that I had with customers and leading programs so, he asked me to become a program manager and it first was kind of funny because I told him, 'No. I don't want to become a program manager.' I didn't like their ethics. I didn't like how they throw engineers under the bus because that was the experience that I had. I quietly declined. They offered me a 20% raise if I would do it so that kind of piqued my ears up and I became a program manager." P03 was reluctant to take the role of program manager initially but was persuaded by leadership based on the qualities that he/she showed and was provided financial incentives to join the program management organization.

All four participants have managed programs with financial responsibilities between 10 to 150 million dollars boundaries. All participants have been working for their current firms for more than 10 years, and three out of the four participants are in the same firm where they started their career after college. The participants' current work locations range from urban to suburban areas. Two of the four participants reside in Illinois, while the remaining two reside in Iowa. All the participants in this study have more than 10 years in program management experience in the aerospace and defense industry and have enjoyed healthy promotion progression through the course of their careers.

Leadership Findings

This section will provide interview data findings from participants based on the leadership skills framework constructs that were established. The leadership skills constructs that were used to explore the demonstration of leadership skills during project execution were emotional intelligent skills, situational leadership skills, relational leadership skills, and transformational leadership skills.

Emotional Intelligent Skills

Participants were asked three questions to explore how they have utilized emotional intelligence skills during the course of their program management career. The three questions were focused on self-awareness, emotional resilience, and sensitivity. During the interview process P01 was asked how self-awareness was demonstrated during the project and what impact it had with the project team. P01 described a situation and stated that, "I was in a room full of engineers, both my company's engineers and my customer's engineers, who were escalating their discussion on a technical point that also intercepted with commercial cost and schedule. The conversation escalated to the point where voices were being raised, shouting, and people were passionate. They were passionate about their position. I vividly remember telling myself I am not allowed to enter into this passionate discussion because, remember, for 16 years I was an engineer. And I had a perspective. I had a viewpoint. But I had to suppress that and say, 'I'm the program manager, everybody else can yell at each other, but I can't. I have to maintain order.' That was one of the distinct moments when although I wanted to engage, I knew that I couldn't and I shouldn't because I had to calm everybody down and return to a more productive discussion. To find a way to get to closure on that topic."

P01 further explained that having the awareness of the personality of the project team was essential to drive a positive outcome from the conversation and solution. P01 also elaborated on the interaction of self-awareness and cultural differences of customers. P01 stated that "Self- awareness becomes more interesting when your customer is a foreign national. When they don't share the same necessarily culture and background that everybody else does. You need to be culturally aware of the fact that the customer's coming from a different perspective than you are." P02 was asked how self-awareness was used during program management experience and P02 explained the importance of understanding and having awareness of cultural differences, especially when dealing with a group or team who are from a different culture.

P02 explained the frustration that other members of the team in United States have with this specific offshore team when it comes to communication and setting expectations. P02 stated that "I recognized the concern on the part of our team, and the frustration on the part of the team in the US, when they weren't getting the answers that they wanted or weren't getting the results that they wanted based on the answers that they were given." P02 was able to use self-awareness to understand the cultural context that the offshore team operate in and was able to communicate with them from a different perspective and get expected results from the offshore team.

P03 also discussed self-awareness as one of the key important aspects of how leaders can effectively lead a project team. When P03 was asked to describe a situation when self-awareness was used to effectively lead a project team, P03 discussed a situation that the relationship between the project team and customer started to deteriorate and it became a toxic relationship. P03 stated that

> we let our emotions start running our project. When I allowed it to happen, the rest of the team, including the engineers and the project support members picked up on those emotions and attitude and then they had that attitude with the supplier and all of a sudden, the team was breaking down and I cannot figure out what is wrong with this team. So, I had to sit down and kind of figure out what was going on and then, as I was talking to the engineering manager about everything we both came to a self-awareness so to speak with each other that we were the problem. The leaders were the problem because we had allowed emotions to take over our business acumen and we were leading the team with emotions rather than with truly leadership and we infected the team. I had to bring the team together and took responsibility for it as the leader of the team and came to head to reset. That was the catalyst that set the recovery and we were back on equal footing with the customer.

P03 discussed the importance of the ability of a leader to control one's own emotions and manage other's emotions. P03 further stated that "I learned as a leader to be self-aware when you are leading the team. It's not just about barking out orders. It's about being self-aware and making sure what you are communicating to the team and more importantly your body language to the team."

When P01 was asked about sensitivity and how it was used to show leadership during the course of the project, P01 elaborated on how a program manager should have a holistic view in sensitivity not only with the internal team, but with external customers and suppliers. P01 says,

> There was a situation that one of the suppliers involved in my production program was in the process of filing for bankruptcy. The customer is also aware of the bankruptcy situation of the supplier and requested for a plan. I made a commitment to provide the plan before the end of the day and I had to work late to accomplish the goal. The customer had a commitment to communicate to their senior leadership to provide updates on the supplier and I was sensitive to the urgency of the need for the plan. The customer was impressed with the fact that I kept my word and provided the information when I said I was going to.

Having sensitivity to the supplier's situation gained P01 well deserved trust with the supplier. P01 stated that "winning the customer's trust is so incredibly vital. But trust is like a crystal goblet. It's so fragile, it can break so easily. So, you need to be careful with it." P01 has been a program manager for about twenty years and described sensitivity as an essential aspect of leadership; being culturally aware is one of the most important aspects of leadership.

P02 explained the importance of sensitivity and how it is essential in the field of project management to get positive results from every member of the organization. P02 discussed a situation where sensitivity was used:

There was an instance where I could tell an employee was upset about or was feeling kind of marginalized in discussions that were occurring. They had been maybe spoken down to a little bit by others on the team. Since we needed the support of every member of the team, I stepped up and recognized the past accomplishments and recent success of the team member to the project and how important new ideas are for the innovation of the project. The body language of the employee immediately changed, and the employee brightened up. The employee continues to be a valuable asset to the team by contributing innovative ideas to solve complex problems.

P02 elaborated on the importance of project members feeling that they are valued and how that contributes to the success of the project.

When P03 was asked how sensitivity was used during the project execution. P03 discussed a situation that involved one of the team members who came into the office in tears because she overheard other team members saying negative things about her. P03 explained how a meeting was set up involving all the team members to discuss the importance of being sensitive to each other's feelings and how inclusion is essential to the spirit of the team. P03 stated, "So, I got the team together and I talked in generalities rather than about her. I just talked about how close a team we are, and how we have to rely on each other." The outcome of the group meeting resulted in the other members of the team apologizing to the offended team member and acknowledged what they did that was wrong. P03 discussed that the situation improved the relationship between the team members and how they continue to work together.

P04 was asked how sensitivity was used to accomplish successful project outcomes. P04 discussed the situation of being sensitive to the skill set of a specific team member and the necessity of putting the resource in a different role to ensure that the resource is thriving and will not leave the organization. P04 stated that the specific resource

> was not necessarily performing in a capacity that's needed as a technical program manager as far as managing the costs and controlling the schedule. I was sensitive to the fact that the resource liked being one of the leaders on the team and instead of removing the resource completely from the team, I talked to the resource to consider a role that is more aligned to the skillset like the program architect and then bring another person to take on the technical program manager role. The resource was happier because it was more of what he would like to do and gave him more freedom and actually more time to dedicate to the technical oversight over the program in the way that could be more helpful.

P04 further explained that being sensitive to team members' needs is essential to getting the best out of the project team and enhancing the successful outcome of the project.

Emotional resilience was explored with participants of the study; participants were asked how emotional resilience was used as one of the key attributes of emotional intelligence to achieve a successful project outcome. P04 discussed the utilization of emotional resilience when there was a poor performance from the project team and the ability to react to the situation in a positive way and be resilient in moving forward with the team to find the right solution for the problem. P04 further explained that the key is to avoid being frustrated based on the issue and focus on how the problems were solved.

P04 stated that "the important thing is how you react to the situation and how you move forward, how you get the team motivated, and overcome whatever poor performance that has happened."

Situational Leadership Skills

Three questions were asked to explore how participants have utilized situational leadership skills during the course of their program management career. The three questions were focused on strategic perspective, critical analysis and judgement, and developing. P01 was asked how strategic perspective was used during the successful management of a program. Understanding the strategy and situation of the customer was very important and P01 further emphasized the importance of understanding the culture of the client. P01 described how situational awareness was used with one of the customers to divert a situation that could negatively jeopardize the relationship between the firm and the customer:

> I had a different customer that was noticeably late in their payments, and we could have suspended shipments but holistically, we understood that was almost like crossing a line that was too much. So, we successfully, 'we' being my team but with me as the point, we successfully convinced the leadership of the customer to make some financial payments in order to avoid us stopping shipments. If I stop the shipment, I will cause damage to the relationship with the customer. Instead of picking the action of stopping the shipment, we improve communication that allows the customer to stop the habit of late payment. The culture of this customer is relaxed with on-time payment, especially at a business and program leadership position.

P01 was able to execute situational leadership skills to understand that the on-time payment maturity level of this particular customer is different from other customers that are more frequent in their payment structure. Having the situational leadership skills to understand the cultural context that the customer was operating in was essential for P01 to successfully lead the program to successful outcome and avoid a situation that could have potentially derailed the program.

P02 explained a situation where strategic perspective was used to develop a better solution for the customer. P02 explained how a proposed design change was made to enhance the future maintainability and sustainability of the product. The decision was not popular due to the increase in design cost, but it was a long-term strategy that had to be made due to the case of the specific customer. P02 further explained that the design proposal was agreed to due to extensive communication of risk impact, maintainability impact, and cost. P02 explained that the outcome of the new design was more attractive, and the organization will continue to use it as a platform for other customers. There has been positive feedback from the customers on the product after understanding the advantages of the new design over legacy product. P02 further discussed the importance of the ability of a program manager to be flexible in making decisions and having a unique view for each customer based on their situation to get the best successful outcome.

P03 explained how critical analysis and judgement was when used during project execution by integrating other team members' ideas during the critical analysis process and prior to making major decisions in the project.

P03 stated "There are times leaders need to make a decision for sure without the team but when I can I have them involved." There was emphasis on involving the team in decision making, which helps sharpen the judgement of P03. P03 described the importance of involving the team in the decision-making process because it helps the team members to feel like they are an integral part of the decision-making, which helps to facilitate buy-in from the team. P03 further stated that "I never try to make a gut decision unless absolutely necessary. I try to think of different ways that I can solve it, think of different outcomes, think of different obstacles that will show up and then pick the best one." The ability of a program manager to explore the advantages/disadvantages of a decision cannot be understated and dealing with each decision based on the situation is one of the key ways that program managers achieve success, according to P03.

When P04 was asked to describe how critical analysis and judgement were used to achieve successful project outcome, P04 discussed how part of the process is to look for recommendations from the team before making decisions and moving forward with a solution. P04 explained the rationale of involving the team in decision making is the ability to have different points of view from several key members to develop key solutions that will meet the customer expectation.

P03 explained the methodology of developing team members to solve complicated problems as a program manager. P03 described "hidden biases" as one of the issues that prevent leaders from developing team members in the organization. P03 further explained the concept of hidden biases as the situation when leaders consistently use their all-star (or experts) to solve problems and ignore the development of other members on the team. P03 described the process of going through self-reflection to avoid "hidden biases" to prevent the development of other members of the team. P03 stated, "I had to recognize hidden biases, when I only look for the expert to solve problems, I'm not looking to other members of the team to help them grow, to help them become that all-star, to help them become that expert. When situations do come up I have to learn to grow other people on a team so I can rely on them equally."

The idea of growing every member of the team equally has been efficient and beneficial to P03, which has helped the project team to be successful in achieving their goals. P04 discussed the process of developing one of the project team members from technical program manager position to a program manager. P04 described how the individual on the team was unsure if she was ready to assume the role of program manager due to lack of experience in managing programs. P04 stated "I provided training to her to ensure that she has knowledge and is comfortable in the position and I established a monthly one-on-one meeting with her to further develop her understanding in program management. The development process created a catalyst of growth for the employee and she was nominated for Engineer of the Year."

Relational Leadership Skills

Two questions were asked to explore how participants used relational leadership skills to lead their project team. The two questions were focused on empowering and engaging communication. When P01 was asked to describe the situation of empowering a team member to accomplish a positive project outcome, P01 stated

> I empowered a new employee from the contract department by teaching her to understand the context of the contract negotiation and trusting her to negotiate the contract by herself. She went into the conference room, just her and the buyer,

nobody else, and I wondered if she was going to be successful or not and she successfully closed the deal. She achieved a better result in the negotiation with the customer, better than what I could have achieved.

P01 explained that empowerment is the combination of mentorship and trust. P01 stated that "after mentoring it is essential to be able to trust them that they were successful in accomplishing the task."

P03 was asked how empowerment was used with the project team to achieve successful project outcome. P03 discussed a situation when there was complicated software that had to be designed by the team. Even though P03 was under severe pressure from the leadership to deliver the software on time, there was a conscious decision to empower the team to decide what type of design would be used for the project. P03 called a meeting with the team and told them: "I'm empowering you to make your own decisions on what you need to do software wise." P03 stated,

> I looked on their calendars and there were meetings going. I sat in a couple of meetings, and I didn't say a word. I let the software team run it. I was just a fly on the wall in the back just kind of listening to them and empowering that team to go off and do what they do best. It was probably the best decision I ever made because they're the ones that actually solved the issue that we had at the time. It was by me getting out of the way that I empowered them to go ahead and make the right decision software wise to do what they needed to be done.

P03 explained that empowering is important and can be challenging for program managers due to the scrutiny of success associated with the completion of projects, but emphasized that it has to be done to ensure that project teams take accountability of the success of the project.

P01 was asked how engaging communication was used to drive successful project outcomes with team members. P01 stated, "Firstly communication is a part of good leadership and efficient communication is an ingredient to be successful as a program manager." P01 described a situation that engaging communication was used with the project team: "There was a case where I had to be very clear in my communication, to say 'this is what we are empowered to do, this is what we are not empowered to do. This is our requirements, this is what I expect, and what the customer needs'." P01 explained that a program manager cannot afford to be ambiguous in communication due to the impact that they have on the success of the team. P01 further elaborated that having the moment of the clear communication was essential in ensuring that every member of the team was operating under the same direction and was consistent in delivering to the objective of the program.

P02 further discussed the importance of engaging communication. P02 discussed a situation of working with an offshore team when the manager had to be clear on the expectations of the project. P02 explained how clarity was provided to the offshore team to allow them to understand project deliverables, what was expected, and design requirements. P02 discussed how there was no room for ambiguity. PO2 used several methods to document the expectation and set up a weekly cadence to ensure that the communicated objectives were being followed. P02 explained that the method of engaging communication resulted in the team having clear understanding on the goals of the project and delivered on the expected result.

Transformational Leadership Skills

Participants were asked three questions to explore how transformational leadership skills were used to gain successful project outcomes during the course of their project execution. The three questions were focused on motivation, influence, and conscientiousness.

When P02 was asked to describe the situation of motivating team members to accomplish a positive result, P02 stated

> A lot of times, I would bring food, especially when we were working long hours. I did try to do a lot of team building activities with the group. We brought the team an outside facilitator to do some team building, just to give them some extra motivation. I was not necessarily trying to be their friend, because I was their boss, but really tried to connect with them and motivate them each individually on how they wanted to be motivated based of their personality. Some of them, it was a compliment on what they've done that day. Some of them, it was joking with them about an issue that they've been dealing with and sharing my concerns or their frustrations.

P02 discussed a classic example of how leaders can effectively motivate teams and also utilize individual consideration to deal with each team members on how they would like to be treated. Individual consideration is an essential skill in the field of project management due to the ability to interact with the project team on a personal level.

McCleskey (2014) explains that leaders use individual consideration to provide a supportive environment for followers that equips followers in reaching their goals and ambitions. When P03 was asked how motivation was used during the project to accomplish successful project outcome, P03 explained that there are three ways that motivation had been used to positively affect the outcome of the project. The first method was to lead by example and lead the team from the front. P03 stated that,

> if my team would have to work late and they're working overtime and giving up family time, I'm here with them. I want them to see that leadership is here also. I'm not just telling them you need to work late and I'll be home you know, watching television and enjoying my family. The second method is to show appreciation and acknowledge their hard work. The third method is to consistently explain the importance why their contribution and their effort is important to the vision of the organization and the customer.

P04 explained the relationship between setting a program vision and motivating the team. P04 stated "I think just setting a vision is a really big deal in motivating a team because they have something to go work for." When a program manager sets a vision and articulates the vision to the team, it makes it easy to motivate the team into buying into the vision and executing the vision. P04 discussed how setting project goals and vision is an essential tool that has been used to successfully motivate the team.

During the interview and data collection, it was noted that the ability to influence internal and external stakeholders is one of the key ways that a program manager can be successful. P01 explained the ability to be proactive in coming up with ideas for team members and leadership, which ensures that people will have to follow the idea that was presented first rather than influencing or convincing the team to adopt a different idea.

P01 stated that "I'm very good at taking an early lead to help shape my program team goals and expectations. As a program manager, I tend to be quick to identify and explain what the goals and expectations are. Consequently, instead of trying to change their mind I've already convinced them through my statements what they should be." P01 shared a different perspective. Instead of influencing, a program manager can lead with ideas and other team members will follow.

Successful Project Outcome Findings

As discussed in Chapter 2, successful project outcome is an essential responsibility of a project manager and reflects the performance of their project. The performance metrics that were used to determine project success criteria followed the Muller and Turner (2007) project success criteria tool. The ten attributes of the project success criteria tool were sent to the organization leadership to confirm that the research participants have a history of managing projects to successful outcomes. The project success criteria documentation was received from the leadership of the four participants' organizations as one of the supportive artifacts and documentation that showed research participants have managed their projects successfully. Figure 12 below shows the supporting artifacts that were received from each participant's leadership. The result of the project success criteria outcome of the four participants who participated in the study shows that they all met the project success criteria as discussed by Muller and Turner (2007).

Candidate Name:		Candidate Email Address:
Project Success Criteria	**Outcome (Yes/No)**	**Notes**
Overall Project Success	Yes	Indicate "Yes" if participants meet the criteria
Meeting User Requirements	Yes	Indicate "Yes" if participants meet the criteria
Meeting Project Purpose	Yes	Indicate "Yes" if participants meet the criteria
Reoccuring Business	Yes	Indicate "Yes" if participants meet the criteria
Customer Satisfaction	Yes	Indicate "Yes" if participants meet the criteria
End-user Satisfaction	Yes	Indicate "Yes" if participants meet the criteria
Stakeholder Satisfaction	Yes	Indicate "Yes" if participants meet the criteria
Supplier Satisfaction	Yes	Indicate "Yes" if participants meet the criteria
Team Satisfaction	Yes	Indicate "Yes" if participants meet the criteria
Self-Defined Success Criteria	Yes	Indicate "Yes" if participants meet the criteria

Figure 12 Successful Project Outcome Confirmation

The four participants were asked to explain if the project that they managed was successful and what their definition of successful project outcome is. This section of research is essential to explore the perspective of each participant on the outcome of the project that they have managed and their understanding of what successful project outcome is. Participants were asked to describe how the project that they've managed is successful and describe their understanding on what project success is.

P01was asked to discuss the definition of project success and to then state if the project managed was successful according to that definition. P01 stated, "My definition of success is meeting the needs of the customer. The customers have a variety of needs that they would want to be met. Through communication you can understand and identify from the customer what are the most important parts of what they need and adapt your program activities to meet those needs." P01 explained that it is important to understand that project success can vary from customer to customer and it typically depends on what is important to the customer. P01 further gave the example that some customers might value project cost over schedule or meeting the scope over cost.

The needs and capabilities that are most important to the customer is what will decide if the project is successful or not successful and it is important for a program manager to know how to prioritize those important attributes in a program. P01 explained one of the ways success can be validated is through customer confirmation. P01 stated that "the customers validated the success of the project by evaluating the statement of work and requirements that were provided against the product that has been delivered to them." P01 further stated that project success in not limited to meeting the external customer's need. P01 explained that meeting the need of the internal customer, which is the organization leadership that the program manager belongs to, is also an essential aspect of successful project outcome. P01 explained other indications that clarified the project that have been managed were successful. P01 elaborated on follow-on projects that were received from the customers due to the relationship and performance on prior projects as a strong indication that the projects managed in the past were successful.

P02 explained the ability to meet the customer's schedule and manage product design that meets the customer's need is a significant aspect of success. P02 stated that "I have been successful in my leadership into my management team. I do feel successful and we've made progress in a lot of the areas in the organization. The fact that I have been asked to take on different roles is an evidence of the recognition of my success in the organization."

When P03 was asked if the projects that have been managed were successful and what the definition of success was, P03 gave a different point of view on what success is at the end of the project. P03 stated, "I look at success as if the team grew, did the team learn from this project? Did they become a better team because of the project? Did they learn something new? Did they learn something new about each other, and was the end customer happy? I always want to grow my teams personally as well as professionally." P03 further explained another method that project success has been validated is by visiting the customer facilities and conducting a one-on-one meeting with the customer and requesting feedback on the products that have been delivered to them.

P04 stated that successful project outcome is "a project that is buildable for the future and a solution that then grows a relationship. Did we do what we said we were going to do? Is it within cost and allotted schedule?" P04 further explained that project success is also the ability to get future business from the customer. P04 stated that one of the driving factors of project success is the ability to gain future business due to the relationship that has been built with the client.

Data Analysis

The interview data showed that the participants in this study used a variety of leadership skills to accomplish successful project outcome. The program managers who participated in this study were responsible in managing the cost, budget, scope, and most importantly the relationship between internal and external customers. The research data further identified that success for these program managers went beyond meeting the customer expectation, but also includes the development of project teams and building long lasting relationships with the customer. Leadership skills utilization was acquired from the participants through semi-structured interviews and successful project execution

history was gathered from the leadership of the participants who participated in the

interview experiment. Within each case, interview questions were posed to the

participants in order to explore the situation in which the leadership skills were utilized

and how the utilization of these skills contributed to successful project outcome.

Participants	Emotional Intelligence Behaviors	Situational Leadership Behaviors	Relational Leadership Behaviors	Transformational Leadership Demonstration
P01	a) Cultural Awareness b) Sensitivity c) Emotional Control	a) Thinking Holistically b) Critical Thinking c) People Development	a) Trust b) Active Communication c) Empowerment d) Clear Expectation	a) Clear Expectation and Goals b) Motivation c) Inspiration d) Influence
P02	a) Cultural Awareness b) Sensitivity c) Emotional Consciousness d) Appreciation	a) Critical Thinking b) Situation Based Solution c) Individual Growth Strategy	a) Sharing Responsibility b) Team Empowerment c) Set Expectation	a) Personalized Motivation b) Influence c) Hardiness
P03	a) Emotional Control b) Personal Reflection c) Emotional Resilience d) Sensitivity Consideration	a) Situation Based Solution b) Critical Thinking c) Team Development	a) Inclusiveness b) Consensus Decision Making	a) Motivation b) Team Appreciation c) Results Oriented d) Motivation
P04	a) Emotional control b) Personal Reflection c) Emotional Resilience d) Sensitivity Consideration	a) People Development b) Skills Awareness	a) Trust and Believe b) Empowerment c) Communication	a) Motivation b) Goals Oriented c) Vision Articulation

Figure 13 Leadership Skills Demonstration Summary

The leadership skills demonstrated in each case are: emotional intelligence,

situational leadership, relational leadership, and transformational leadership skills. The

data gathered during the interview process showed consistency in leadership skills

utilization among the four participants to ensure successful project outcome in most

cases. One of the main responsibilities of a project manager is to lead a group of people

who do not necessarily directly report to them as discussed in this study. None of the

participants have any resource that directly reports to them, but they are responsible to lead multiple resources to accomplish the completion of a given project. Leading multiple teams with limited direct authority requires emotional intelligence skills to sustain the ability to manage other people's emotions and control one's own emotions, especially when dealing with a complex project. The participants in this study demonstrated emotional intelligence by being confident in their interpersonal skills, self-confidence, and self-awareness. These emotional intelligence attributes have helped the participants create vibrant working environments and gave them the ability to manage individuals with various personalities throughout the process of a project. The participants in this research study demonstrated situational leadership skills by utilizing situational based approach to manage their customers and team to successful project outcome.

P01 and P02 explained that the awareness of cultural differences is one of the most important aspect of self-awareness that was utilized during the course of the project to accomplish successful project outcome. Self-awareness is one of the important attributes of emotional intelligence skills, which is a key leadership skill that project management should have due to the level of interaction that exists between them and multiple people. The emphasis of having cultural awareness is essential for project managers who work in a global scale and must communicate with people from different backgrounds. Cultural awareness is beyond working with people from different ethnic backgrounds; however, it also involves having the awareness of different areas of specialty that a project manager is engaging with on a daily basis. Having self-awareness helped the participants in this study to understand the context that they are operating in and how to manage the emotions of their project team to accomplish successful project outcomes. This research data showed how program managers must engage with hundreds of people with different specialties, and the ability to have awareness helped them to be successful.

Being sensitive is one of the essential characteristics of emotional intelligence leadership skills that the participants in this study used to accomplish successful project outcomes. According to the interview data, the relationship between the program managers and the project team significantly improved after the program managers demonstrated that they were sensitive of the feelings and the needs of their project team members. The demonstration of sensitivity by these program managers helped their project team to be willing to work harder and achieve project objectives.

Chapter Summary

The results of the qualitative data were conclusive and answered the research questions to explore the contribution of leadership skills for successful project outcomes. Prior to the start of the interview process, participants received and signed consent forms that informed them of their anonymity and confidentiality. All participants were also informed of the right to withdraw from the study at any point. The research study explored how emotional intelligent skills, situational skills, relational skills, and transformational leadership skills contribute to successful project outcome. Participants were asked leadership questions that helped to explore the leadership skills that they have utilized during their career in project management. The results displayed that the participants were program managers according to their job title and had experience managing multiple projects simultaneously. Furthermore, 50% of the participants were female and 50% were male. All participants have graduate degrees in either engineering or business management with more than 10 years of professional experience in the field of project management.

The second section emerged from the semi-structured interview questions that were used to collect data related to the practice of leadership from the participants. The leadership questions were divided into four leadership theories of emotional intelligence skills, situational leadership skills, relational leadership skills, and transformational leadership skills. The third section of the research was focused on exploring the perception of the participants on what project success is and their understanding of how their projects have been successful through their project management career. All questions were answered by participants via teleconference to explore the contribution of leadership skills in successful project managers.

Chapter V

Summary

Discussion and Implications of Study

The purpose of this qualitative multi-case study was to understand the impact that leadership skills in project managers have on successful project outcome. The research study also explored the leadership skills in project managers and set out to understand how the practice of these leadership skills contribute to successful project outcome in the aerospace and defense industry. Aerospace and defense project managers operate in a tense and challenging environment and it is imperative for them to have effective leadership skills to succeed in this environment. Lack of utilization of leadership skills has caused project failures which have resulted in loss of customer confidence, capital overrun, and an unhealthy work environment. The outcome of this study was based on the exploration of the perspective of selected program managers and additional documentation from their employers that confirmed each participant had history of managing projects to successful outcome.

The research data of emotional intelligence skills has theoretical implication and align with what literature discussed on the importance of the demonstration of emotional intelligence skill. Walker (2008) and Trejo (2016) explained the correlation between leaders who can regulate their emotions with the ability to manage the moods of their followers and described people with high emotional intelligence as having the ability to exhibit a positive emotional outlook to reduce the amount of negativity in the organization. Self-awareness will help leaders to understand self-worth, which will improve self-efficacy in the process of project leadership (Trejo, 2016). Literature further explained that self-awareness is one of the most important attributes of emotional intelligence skills that is essential for program managers (Turner & Lloyd-Walker, 2008; Day et al., 2008). Trejo (2016) further explained that people with high emotional intelligence have the ability to exhibit a positive emotional outlook to reduce the amount of negativity in the organization, which improves successful productivity in the organization.

The program managers who were involved in this study also utilized situational leadership skills during the course of their project management careers, which contributed to their overall success. The research data showed the importance of a program manager possessing awareness of what is important to each customer and cultural traits to ensure that there will be success in the dealings with the customer. This study showed that each customer is different and for a program manager to be successful, he or she must approach each customer based on that customer's maturity level and the situation.

Literature explained that situational leadership encourages leaders to see each task or situation differently and modify his or her leadership strategy based on a given task or situation (Lynch et al., 2011). McCleskey (2014) further explained that having situational leadership skills is the ability of a leader to understand the appropriate response and strategy to employ in any given situation. The participants of this study demonstrated situational leadership skills by individualizing their strategies with cultural awareness, which contributed to successful project outcome. The data gathered in this study showed that situational leadership skills are essential to adapt and lead each program based on the context and situation of the customer.

Relational leadership skill empowers individuals in an organization by sharing responsibility and giving people a sense of ownership in the organization (Martin, Liao, & Campbell, 2013; Raffo, 2012). Literature further discussed that empowerment is one of the key attributes of relational leadership skills as described by Raffo (2012). Program managers who consistently empower project team members will see innovative ideas developed. The research data shows that the program managers who participated in this study were successful due to their ability to empower, trust, and create an inclusive environment for their project team. The research data shows how the program managers who participated in the study empowered and trusted their project team to make decisions without micro-managing the process of the decision. The impact of empowering their project team to make independent decisions resulted in their project team's ability to come up with an innovative solution which resulted in the successful project outcome.

The practical implication of empowering and trusting a project team to make project decisions is the innovative growth that it fosters in project team members and the creation of lasting relationships between team members. When team members feel included in the team decision making it enables them to be invested in the decision and take ownership in the accomplishment of the project goal.

Literature further confirmed the importance of the findings on relational leadership skills by describing the importance of inclusiveness in understanding the diversity that exists with people and creating a relationship that accomplishes mutual goals with individual incorporation point of view (Fairhurst & Uhl-Bien, 2012;

Hollander, 2009). One of the practical implications of the utilization of relational leadership skills by the program managers in this study is the innovative skills that were created through empowerment that enhance successful project outcome.

This research data shows how essential transformational leadership skills are in the field of project management and how the participants in the study used this skill set to accomplish successful project outcome. The research demonstrated the importance of a program manager to be motivated and influence skills. The program managers who participated in this study motivated their team, especially during technically challenging situations, to accomplish successful project outcomes. These program managers where able to motivate their project teams by leading from the front, which resulted in their ability to meet their stakeholder's goals.

The research data also highlighted how influencing skill is essential to accomplish successful project outcome. The program managers in this study were able to influence their project team and all stakeholders to adopt their vision of the program, which resulted in successful completion of their project. The importance of transformational leadership skills cannot be understated in the field of project management. Literature explained that transformational leadership skill sets instill optimism and motivation to encourage team members to achieve a common goal (Nixon et al., 2012; McCleskey, 2014). Literature further explained that transformational leadership skills can be used to improve a follower's performance through a common commitment beyond an individual goal and set management effectiveness (Byman et al., 2011; McCleskey, 2014).

Summary

This study was based on an exploration to understand how leadership skills contribute to successful project outcomes by project managers. Each program manager has his/her own perspective on how they utilized leadership skills to achieve a successful project outcome. It is important to also note the similarities between the four cases. Three out of the four cases emphasized cultural awareness as one of the most important skills that helped to successfully lead teams on a global scale. All participants discussed the importance of empowering the project team and how this was used as a catalyst to spur innovation in solving complex problems.

The participants in this study did not mention their technical background or expertise as one of the driving factors that enable them to have successful project outcomes. This was an interesting observation since all the participants have strong engineering backgrounds. The research data shows that program managers attributed their project success with their leadership skills rather than their technical knowledge or background. Another key observation from the research data is that majority of the participants do not have a project management certification. There is only one out of the four participants who has project management certification; however, all of the participants have had multiple project management trainings at some point in their career. This observation shows that having a project management certification could be useful to be a project manager, but leadership skills are needed to be a successful project leader, especially in the aerospace and defense industry.

This study gained insight on understanding how leadership skills contributed to successful project outcome by successful project managers. Both literature review and interview data collected from participants showed there's a significant role leadership plays in the field of project management and the ability of a leader to utilize leadership skills will contribute to a successful project outcome. The results and practical implication of this study are useful to enlighten organizations that leadership skills are needed and contribute to successful project outcomes of complex projects.

Assumptions and Limitations

This research study assumed that the four participants included in the research study answered the interview questions accurately and openly based on their knowledge and experience. The participants of this study were limited to project managers in the aerospace and defense industry, which means that the findings and results are only limited within the context of this specific industry.

Another form of personal limitation of this research study is bias that could have been introduced through the usage of personal contact to reach participants. This limitation was mitigated by ensuring that organization leadership provided documentation that a nominated participant is a successful project manager by completing the successful project outcome by Muller and Tuner (2007). The limited participants of this research study is another form of limitation to obtain more than is currently available. This limitation was mitigated by the utilization of triangulation of documentation from organization leadership to confirm that candidates are successful project managers.

Recommendations for Future Research

The data of the research study provided information on the implication and impact of the practice of leadership skills in successful project outcomes. This study was a four multiple-case study and the participants have deep technical and engineering experience. Even though the research data does not indicate that the successful project outcome of the program managers is enhanced by their technical skills, exploring leadership skills of program managers without technical background could be important. This type of study would help to understand similar leadership skills with program managers without or with limited technical background to understand if there is an impact on their successful project outcomes. The results of this type of study could also be used for comparison between program managers with technical backgrounds and without technical backgrounds to understand if there are differences in successful project outcomes. Another recommendation for future research is the qualitative study of program managers that have been unsuccessful and the exploration of leadership skills of team members within a project.

www.ingramcontent.com/pod-product-compliance
Lightning Source LLC
LaVergne TN
LVHW041333200726
843509LV00009B/699